YOU'VE EARNED IT!

YOU'VE EARNED IT!

HOW I REFUSED ANYTHING LESS THAN SUCCESS
(AND YOU CAN TOO)

CHRIS ROBERTS

OBD BOOKS

ISBN-13: 978-1-7330229-0-3

ISBN-10: 1-7330229-0-2

This book is dedicated to Ron and Margie Norgan.

If not for your guidance, support, mentorship, and acceptance, I cannot imagine what direction my life would have gone. It is my greatest wish that everyone has the opportunity to be influenced by wonderful people like you at some point in their lives. Thank you for changing my life.

CONTENTS

YOU'VE EARNED IT!

INTRODUCTION

T HIS IS NOT one of those quick-fix books on how to change your life in one week. Nor is this a "How to Get Rich by Following My Lead" program. However, this *is* my real-life example of how one individual overcame tremendous adversity at a very young age to eventually become truly happy and effective in his personal and professional life. I will detail some of the tools I utilized along the way and demonstrate how the average or even below-average person can accomplish great things.

Today I run a multimillion-dollar sales and marketing company, and a successful real-estate and rental business. I've won many awards. I was a decorated volunteer reserve police officer for four years. And I'm happily married.

By every measure, I should not be where I am today. I was born to fifteen-year-old parents—still kids themselves—and largely raised by my single mother. I lived a nomadic childhood, which included standing in the occasional free food line and living off food stamps for most of it. I slept on the sofas of anyone who would take

1

me in, including friends and family, and eventually moved out on my own at the age of fifteen. I did not go to college. I did not even graduate from high school.

I wrote this book because I wanted to share my thoughts with those individuals who feel they don't have a chance in life to succeed. Maybe you've reached a roadblock you're having trouble climbing over. Or you've had a hard life or no support system in place to keep you on track. This book is also for the parent who wants to share a story with their child who just can't seem to straighten out. It's for anyone down on their luck and unable to get out of a rut.

Getting what you want in your personal and professional life can be an overwhelming thought. There is a reason so few people achieve true wealth, work at a job they love, and get to retire early. But if you change your way of thinking, invest in yourself, and work hard, you will open yourself to new opportunities.

I can't tell you how many times I achieved a goal or made extra money or won an award or got a job or you fill in the blank because I literally outworked everyone around me. See, not having the education, family status, or basically any leg up, I had to find my own way. I worked, played, and volunteered with a lot of people who were smarter, stronger, and more skilled than me, that's for sure. But one unique thing I had going for me was a relentless pursuit to excel and prove to others that I was worthy. I knew if I could grind, push, hustle, listen and learn, help others, and just basically outwork people around me, I would have a chance.

The key here is setting goals and regularly measuring them. To look at it another way, if you work for a company, they will set goals higher than they think you can reach. They do this knowing that they will reach a higher number than where they started and it's likely it will be *close* to the goal. There is only one Bill Gates, one Richard Branson, one Tony Robbins, and so on, but there are *millions* of successful people between you and them that are reaching their goals every day while building wealth and happiness. Don't stress about the overwhelming thought of your goals being too high, the failures that may come along on your journey, or what anyone thinks about your dream.

Just get inspired and don't look back.

CHRIS ROBERTS

CHAPTER ONE

KID BEING RAISED BY KIDS

F ROM THE MOMENT I was born, I lived with multiple family members, moving from place to place. My mother and father, Donna and Tom, were barely freshmen in high school when my life began in 1977. All they could think about was rock music and smoking weed. Now they were faced with the very adult responsibility of a baby. I can't imagine how difficult a challenge it must have been—two young people who are not even responsible enough to be on their own now faced with the reality of raising a baby. My dad was in the picture occasionally on weekends, but was never there full-time as a father. He tried the best he could, but it must have been overwhelming for him.

I can remember several of my mother's friends we stayed with and all the strange people who came and went on a regular basis. One specific neighborhood we lived in was across the street from Disneyland in Anaheim, California, but this neighborhood was no Disneyland. I saw things children should not see and heard things children should not hear.

For instance, I always looked forward to the sound of the ice-cream truck coming through our neighborhood, even though it was rare that we had the money to buy ice cream for ourselves. But having the ice-cream truck's bells in the air was a welcome break from the day-to-day poverty and usual boredom. That all came to a halt one day when the ice cream man was arrested for selling methamphetamine along with his tasty pops. It was a long while before we'd see any ice-cream man again.

Another time, my mother awoke in the middle of the night to find a strange man standing over her bed with her jewelry box in one hand and a screwdriver in the other. She screamed at the top of her lungs, startling the intruder, who ran out of her room, through the front door, and down the alley. She still tells the story of screaming at the top of her lungs as she ran out the front door after the intruder. She saw a neighbor and cried for help, but to no avail, as people minded their own business in our rough neighborhood, and for good reason.

I can only imagine what that intruder thought, because my mother was a tough redhead and certainly not someone you would consciously steal jewelry from. He's *lucky* he ran. I was no more than five years old at the time.

There were a ton of crime and theft and bad people around us, but I did not know any different. It was my normal.

Between the ages of five through eleven, my regular memories include frequenting biker bars with Mom, rock bands playing in the apartment, motorcycles being worked on in the living room, others' constant smoking and drinking and even drugs, though they tried to hide it from me. There were neighbors with names like Snake and Butch. Mom's friends were dying of drug overdoses or in motorcycle accidents. And there was the occasional table being thrown through the glass door by a drunk boyfriend.

When I was about seven years old, there was an apartment building we lived in with one of my aunts where all the neighboring mothers were in a clique and unwilling to accept new single mothers into their group. As strange as this may sound, in many neighborhoods, you were either in or you were out.

My mother was very protective of me. We didn't have a lot, but she loved me and always fiercely stood up for me. I remember one of the ladies in this clique made fun of me one day. My mother calmly asked my aunt Vicki to take me inside the apartment and then confronted the bully. In response, the woman who made the mean comments pushed my mother—only to regret it. My mother reared back and punched this lady, taking her to the ground and tearing her shirt apart. "Never disrespect my son again, or next time you'll get it far worse!" my mom promised. She was twenty-two years old.

Now some people might look at that as a terrible way to raise a child and by no means a good way to set an example. But throughout the years, living in some of our neighborhoods, this was a regular occurrence and very much normal. I was scared while all this was going down and would not fully understand the scope of what my mother did for me until my later years. I am grateful today that she was so protective and always willing to stand up for us.

In thinking back about the first seven years of my life, the only good memories I had were my mother defending us on a regular basis and doing her best to make me feel safe, the unconditional love of my maternal grandma, Cleone, and the time I made $1.50 selling lemonade with the neighborhood kids on the corner. That was my first taste of entrepreneurship.

By nine, I was living with my aunt in a different part of Anaheim and attending the third grade. Mom would stay as much as she could, but there was not a lot of room. I remember the sounds of helicopters (or as Ice Cube would call them, "Ghetto Birds") flying overhead with their spotlights on. They did this when the police were searching for people who had committed violent crimes in the city. There was a drill when you heard or saw them coming—drop everything, get inside, and lock the doors.

While living there I can vividly remember watching gangs regularly beat people up in my neighborhood and being thankful that they did not take interest in me. One time I watched a gang of four girls beat up another girl so badly that she was knocked unconscious. They all laughed as they walked away, leaving the victim lying in the bushes. I was so shocked at what I saw that all I could do was crouch down across the street and hide.

I tried to fit in when we moved from place to place by being funny. This got me in trouble in class but worked on the playground, at least sometimes. I'm not even sure why I was funny; I just remember making people laugh and that felt good. Thinking back about that time in my life, I was developing my personality and kind of figuring out how to connect with other kids. Due to my circumstances, I never felt like I fit anyplace or had anyone that I could truly identify with. What was I to say? "Hi, I'm the nomadic poor kid living on my aunt's couch and I will most likely be moving soon."

I knew I did not fit in because sometimes I would overhear kids' parents making comments about me and where I lived or what I did not have.

One day while playing on the school grounds with a rare friend, we were approached by two girls and two older boys. One of the boys started yelling at me that I was looking at them the wrong way. He then punched me in the face, which split my lip. The fifth-grade boy was huge compared to me and I did nothing to deserve a punch to the face. But that's how it goes, I guess. I have the scar to this day under my upper lip as a reminder.

While riding bikes with another friend at that same school, we were confronted by two young adults, one on the handlebars of the other's bike. He jumped off the handlebars and grabbed my bike. "If you don't give me this bike, I will kill you," he said. I was scared to death to put it mildly. Without hesitation, I gave up the bike and watched them ride off. It was bad enough that the bike I was riding was just stolen by two thugs, but to add insult to injury, the bike wasn't even mine. It was my best friend's. We'd switched bikes that day for fun…and the day ended up anything but fun.

Sorry, Damien (my friend's name).

His mom was so angry she would not allow Damien and I to be friends anymore. It was not my fault, but she never forgave me for giving up her son's bike. It was not fair for her to blame me, but there no such thing as fair. There's just life, as I would learn repeatedly during the next several years.

At school I was often picked on by several popular kids, including one boy who would not leave me alone. One day I was so fed up that I said something back to him before class. It felt good, but after school, in retaliation, I was cornered by several boys and they forced me to fight my nemesis. The only problem was I did not know how to fight. After we rolled around a bit, I got punched several times before the fight was broken up by a teacher. My defeat was very embarrassing and set the tone for a low point in my childhood. After having several bikes stolen, always being picked on and made fun of, and then getting beat up, I wished to give up, at the ripe old age of nine.

That night my mom could tell something was wrong and she persisted in getting it out of me. I broke down and told her I did not want to be here anymore. I felt so alone, so broken. I cried as I pleaded with her to make them like me. I couldn't understand why kids didn't like me. Why did I get beat up and made fun of? All these years of witnessing violence, living in poverty, and being picked on were taking their toll.

My mom was devastated but she stayed strong. Wrapped in her arms, she reassured that it was not about me, it was them, and that I had nothing to be ashamed of. She also promised it would pass. I do not remember what else we discussed, but I remember we both cried and made it through.

Afterward, I took her words to heart, but a lonely restlessness remained.

While living in Anaheim I once acted out with some kids, stupidly ripping out bamboo trees at a neighboring complex. I remember being taken to my aunt's in the back of a police car and crying like crazy. This was the first time I had been in real trouble. Thankfully I learned a valuable lesson about respecting the authorities that day. I will never know if I was just being a normal kid, or if there was a deeper issue, but at the time it was just fun to destroy something and rebel. Aside from the helicopters, gangs, and violence, I most remember living off rice with canned gravy (my aunt's favorite), sugar bread (this was a regular dessert for me), and just waiting every two weeks for our food stamps to come. Seriously, getting close to food stamp day was the most exciting thing in my life for a long time. I never went completely hungry, but we always cut it so close. I'm forever grateful to Aunt Vicki for taking care of me the best she could.

Later, my aunt Cindy offered to let me stay with her. Cindy did not have any children of her own, but I shared the home with her boyfriend and his son, who was about my same age. For the first time in my life I had someone who was almost like a brother, in the sense that we were peers and could hang out and support each other. Living with Aunt Cindy was the most structured part of my childhood until about the sixth grade. We lived in a modest home in a good neighborhood. I had a fresh outfit laid out for me every day for me and had to do my homework before anything else after school. Cindy took us to Knotts Berry Farm and other family fun places and really tried to make us feel like a family. I particularly remember Cindy taking me by the doughnut shop many mornings before school. Man, that was awesome.

Unfortunately, the welcome new normal didn't last forever. I'm not sure why, but I assume my aunt and mother had a serious disagreement, because I was once again on my way to another place.

CHAPTER TWO

OPPORTUNITY PRESENTS ITSELF

W HEN I WAS IN the fourth grade, a friend's mother, who worked for a candy factory, brought home several trays of extra Christmas candy.

"Chris, would you like a tray to take home to your family?" she asked.

I grabbed that tray of candy before she could finish her sentence. Each tray had approximately fifty to sixty candies wrapped in decorative holiday foil. Even at a young age, my entrepreneur instinct kicked in. They were perfect for resale. Most of the kids attending elementary school were given change for the pay phone if needed, or simply for extra snacks at school. I took that candy to a thriving "marketplace" and sold almost all of it for twenty-five cents each, netting almost thirteen dollars— more money than I'd ever had. That is until the teacher caught on to my successful exchange and called my mother. Unfortunately, this story does not end well. I lost all my profits, the inventory, *and* was grounded, to cap off what started as a great day.

So much for capitalism.

After my mother met who would turn out to be her future husband, Dave, we all moved in to an apartment together and began what appeared to be a normal life in another bad neighborhood. Dave was an okay stepdad, but he had a drinking problem. It did not directly affect me but he was often in a bad mood and listened to Metallica at about one hundred decibels, blowing my ears out on a regular basis. Like my young parents, I don't think he really knew how to raise a kid. In only their midtwenties, they were still too close to being kids themselves, and just starting to learn life responsibilities.

In looking back at this point in my life I reflect on another entrepreneurial opportunity that presented itself. I wanted things like toys and candy—you know, *kid priorities*. My mother said to me, "If you want something, you have to earn it. We don't have money for things that are not priorities."

How do you earn it at the age of nine? I thought to myself after she explained what priorities meant.

While hanging with a friend, I saw a guy washing his car in the complex. I liked the look of it—a yellow sports car. I asked if he needed any help and he said sure. When my friend and I were done helping the man wash his car, he gave us each a dollar. *This is crazy,* I thought. *He gave us a dollar for washing his cool car!* I was happy to simply be associated with such a cool car, let alone *get paid for it!*

An idea was born.

That weekend I had cars lined up for washing and hired my friend as my first employee. I made at least forty dollars and thought I was on the way to untold riches—that is until the landlord of the apartment complex confronted my mother with the potential water cost and a command to stop immediately. Luckily, my mother let me keep the money after giving my friend his fair cut. The landlord cooled down and chalked it up as a life lesson learned. I will never know if a desire to have things, a chance encounter with a cool car, my mother's comments, or just dumb luck should be credited as the reason I built my car washing empire that day. But one thing is for sure—I liked the feeling of earning something for myself.

A CHANGE IS ON THE HORIZON

At about the age of eleven, we moved to a new city in Southern California. My mother, stepfather and I lived in a small two-bedroom apartment on a street that bordered Santa Ana. The area was rife with gang activity. My mother wasn't the perfect role model but something I do remember her saying early and often was "Don't do drugs and don't join a gang." Her words stuck even when some of my peers would later do the opposite. Drugs offered potential comfort and a sense of acceptance with my peers and gangs offered security, yet my mom is a fierce redhead whom I feared far more than the acceptance of gangs, peer pressure, or pleasures promised using drugs.

When I joined middle school, I was again the new kid on the block. It took a little time to meet friends, but eventually I found a few. Many of the kids I became friends with either lived close to the school or on the east side in the nicer neighborhoods. The first day of school I can remember being made fun of by a group of kids because of the unpopular shoes I wore. They were Pro Wings sneakers from Payless, and only poor kids wore Pro Wings. Most of the other kids sported Nikes or Vans.

Man, how I wanted a pair of Vans shoes.

Here we go again . . . another place where everybody makes fun of me.

But eventually I settled in with those few friends I made—riding bikes and starting to feel somewhat normal. The first few months I lived there I met a boy who lived in the apartment complex behind me. His mother was also a single parent. He was fortunate because his mother set him up with the Big Brothers of America, an organization that provides older mentors to help kids of single parents with guidance and structure. I remember thinking how cool it must be to have an older brother to teach you things, offer a sense of protection, and take you places.

I had the great fortune of meeting a few nice kids on the east side of town through school that were good influences and hung out with them regularly. One of these kids, Marshall, lived in a big house with a swimming pool and it was my mission in life to try to stay at Marshall's house whenever possible. Marshall was a blond-haired, blue-eyed kid, who was smart and athletic. He had great parents and everything going for him. I never quite understood why Marshall was such a good friend of mine, as I had nothing to offer him. We were total opposites, yet he and his kind mom always welcomed me.

I learned a lot about compassion and acceptance from Marshall and his family and will never forget the way they invited me into their home and lives. Maybe it was because I was a funny kid or maybe they just felt sorry for me. Who knows? It didn't matter. All the cute girls would come over and swim at Marshall's, and *that* was cool because cute girls never wanted to hang out at my house.

But danger was never far away. After six months settling in, I was faced with my first encounter with gangs. I was walking home and saw a group of five boys hanging out on my street. Naively, I approached and asked what they were up to and if I could hang with them. I will never forget what happened next. One, ironically named Angel, said to the other boys, "Get him and kick his ass!"

I was like: "What did I do?" They surrounded me and I was punched and kicked dozens of times all over my body by five gang members just for being in the wrong place at the wrong time. In fact, I was kicked in the head so many times that not a single place on my head would be clear of a bump the width of a Nike Cortez toe—the shoe every one of them wore. I was so scared all I could think was, *I'm going to die today.* This was the first but certainly not the last time I would be jumped by gang members near my home in Southern California.

I was eleven years old.

Welcome to my childhood.

After one minute it was over, but it felt like an eternity. I remember them telling me that I was in their gang now, and my first thought was, *My mother is going to kill me.* Why would I want to be friends with a group of people that just beat me like crazy? I was devastated and really roughed up. I went home and cried because I was so embarrassed and scared. Of course I couldn't hide that I was beat up, but I didn't tell my mom it was done by a gang.

I was approached by an older boy later that same week in the neighborhood. He said he was the leader of the gang that jumped me and that they did not want me in their gang. If anyone asked, I was to say I just got beat up by his gang and that I'm not in it. I was happy but confused. Was I so pathetic that a gang didn't even want me after they beat me up to bring me in? I must admit that I was relieved because at the time the one thing I feared more than gangs was my mother. Not having to tell her about "joining" was a big deal.

Being a kid can be so confusing. I have no idea how I made it through my first fifteen years, but I can tell you that all these challenges definitely made a difference in who I am today.

A few months after being jumped. I was walking home with a friend who lived in the apartments behind us. We were excitedly discussing our brand-new toy cars that our mothers had just gifted. They had all kinds of cool parts that you could customize and trade.

As we rounded the corner, my heart sank. A group of boys were huddled together across the street—never a good sign. Immediately, four of the boys crossed the street in our direction.

"Hey, what's that in your hand?" one asked.

I replied that it's a new toy car my mom just bought for me. Another of the boys asked if he could see it, and I said, "Sure, just be careful, it's new." He took the car and walked away. Annoyed, I asked him for my car back and he yelled profanities at me. All four boys stared menacingly.

As fear started rising in me, all I could think about was if I could make it to my apartment, I'd be safe. My friend and I turned to leave but before we could proceed I was surrounded by the four boys. And they only wanted me, not my friend, for some reason. *Here we go again.* . . . The boy who took my car, who was the smallest of the group, suddenly punched me in the face. I took off toward my apartment, yet before I knew it they had me up against a parked car, punching and kicking me. I remember the feeling of my head bouncing off the window frame of the car door several times. I felt as though I was going to pass out. As fearful tears started running down my face, a sense of sheer survival instinct sparked. I swung my arm back and must've knocked one of them down because a hole opened and I was able to run to my apartment. I ran inside, as my friend followed, asking, "Are you okay?" I was bleeding and still crying hysterically. I was out of my mind—so angry that they had taken something so special from me and then beat me up for absolutely no reason. And there was *nothing* I could do about it. I could not control my emotions. I could not understand *why* they would do this to me. My friend left as I called my mother.

Afterward, something snapped. I grabbed my mom's baseball bat and ran outside, screaming and yelling, "I'll get all you &^$*%#!" They all ran and disappeared like cockroaches into the surrounding apartments. Soon thereafter my mother rushed home from work. She was very upset over the incident and spoke to the landlord, but unfortunately the landlord was the grandmother of one of the boys. We found my ruined car at the bottom of their pool. I felt humiliated and embarrassed that I had lost a toy my mom worked very hard to purchase for me. My mother considered calling the police, but didn't want to make matters worse for me, as I had to go to school with these same boys. Besides, what would the police do? They were dealing with far more serious issues in our neighborhood.

One evening while playing on the apartment complex's driveway with some friends, we observed a mini truck slowly driving through the neighborhood. The side window of the canopy slid open and a shotgun was pointed out. I remember someone yelling, "What gang do you claim?" as they drove through, but lucky for us the shotgun was pulled inside and they continued on. On another day I witnessed a skinhead gang fighting with a Mexican gang. All parties involved were swinging chains, baseball bats, and sticks. Many people got severely injured, and it was nothing I would want to see again. These types of incidents happened several times while I lived on the border of two cities.

After several encounters with gangs and bullies in my rough neighborhood, I developed a clever way of getting in and out of my apartment as to avoid confrontation. I would sneak out of the backyard and climb up on the carport behind our apartments, then I would run along the carports and exit on the block behind us. This way I avoided being jumped out front on the main street where they gathered. I did this constantly to and from school and eventually found other clever ways to avoid gangs or mean groups of kids.

CHAPTER THREE

NEW FRIENDS

M Y SCHOOL was very diverse. We had all walks of life. One friend I met, whose name was Reggie, taught me how to dance. I remember how cool it was that people clapped when we would perform dance moves like the Kid 'n' Play, Roger Rabbit, Running Man, or just breakdance on a sheet of cardboard. (Eventually I would learn to dance in general and get pretty good at it.)

Reggie was a truly good person and did not judge people. He was one of the first to help me start building my confidence at school. I then met several kids who liked to ride bikes, so my mother and grandmother Cleone purchased one for me. Finding kids to relate to was critical to getting over being beat up and picked on. I found I had to work hard to find the right group, but once I did, it made a world of difference for me.

There was another kid, Matt, who was one grade higher but hung out with our bike-riding group. He was tough; he studied martial arts and had been in several fights by the eighth grade. I was influenced by the confidence and independence he had. Nobody messed with Matt. I really wanted to study martial arts, so I could be like him and hopefully nobody would mess with me. I didn't have the cash for martial arts classes, but I soon found an opportunity to earn some money by starting a paper route. It didn't pay a lot, but what I earned was mine. I would get up early on the weekends to work and delivered papers after school on weekdays. I think I made about thirty dollars a month, which at the time felt like a fortune. We had the chance to earn extra prizes if we signed up new customers going door to door. I took advantage of that every chance I could. Ultimately, I used the money I made—along with several family members' support—to join a martial arts class.

Things went great while learning martial arts until my bike was stolen outside the dojo. But I didn't let that get me down, as I was learning martial arts and soon would be tough like Matt. Martial arts taught me discipline, accountability, and, above all things, how to take a punch without running and crying.

BONUS POINT: It's important when growing up to make friends with all walks of life: black, white, Asian, Mexican, thick, thin, tall, short, gay or straight, physically or mentally disabled, or other. Don't judge people, as you likely know nothing about them and their circumstances. Be your best and honest and true to the friends that embrace you. Understand that when you're young, things may happen to you that make no sense or that you cannot explain, but don't take it personally. Chances are the issue is with the people on the other side, not you. One of those diverse kids may make an enormous difference in your life, but you must me open to all types of kids and be willing to accept everyone into your heart and learn from those friendships. Stand up for people who are having a tough time standing up for themselves. Do that and others will have your back too.

One day after school I noticed my upstairs window was oddly left open. I soon found that my stepdad had climbed through the window. He normally worked until four p.m. every day, so I wondered why he was home early and—more importantly—why he did not go through the front door. Later that night I learned that he had been drinking at work and was asked to leave his job. On the way home, he struck a parked car around the corner from our apartment and totaled his own car. This recurring behavior eventually caused him to lose his job. The event would put our family into a compromising position and force us to move yet again.

Soon I was on my way to live with my aunt Vicki again. This was an extra struggle for my mom because due to her job's location she would not live with me, but would drive forty-five miles each way (my aunt did not drive) just to keep me in the same middle school. To help lift the burden, I stayed with friends close to my school as much as I could. This was all I could do to feel normal and help my mom with travel issues. One night while staying at a friend's house I overheard his mother saying, "Why is he here all the time? Doesn't he have a home of his own? It's one more mouth to feed." And a few other choice comments.

I was thirteen. This was devastating for a kid my age. All I ever wanted was to fit in and be like everybody else. I didn't *ask* to stay there all the time. My friend wanted me to stay and I was invited. I appreciated the opportunity, but what his mother said crushed me and I would never stay there again. The funny thing is this family was wealthy and had ten times what my mom and I had. But it was clear—I wasn't welcome anymore.

BONUS POINT: To people who have nothing encouraging or positive to say, please be aware that you can affect a child's life forever if you're not careful. I was fine, eventually, but at that point in my life it was extremely difficult for me, and I was very impressionable. And to children who are the recipient of a careless adult's criticism, don't take it personally. I know that will be hard, but you have done nothing wrong and you have a wonderful life waiting out there for you. Stay positive and be your best you.

As eighth grade came to an end and I prepared for my freshman year at high school, a boy named Roy talked to me about playing football. I had never played an organized sport before, but thought it would be fun to join and make friends. I told Roy that I would love to try out for football, but I didn't have a place to live in the school district and I didn't think my mom could afford the mandatory football training camp. By the next day, Roy's mom called mine and generously offered to let me live with them, so I could play football and have a place to stay close to my friends.

The ultimate arrangement was that Roy's mom would give me a place to stay and my mom would pay for my football camp. It's hard to imagine how one mother can have so much compassion for a friend of her son while another could have so much disdain, referencing the earlier example. But one thing was clear: Roy's mom treated me like a son and loved me like her own. And that was very comforting.

Football was a turning point in my life; it got me in shape, plus taught me responsibility and the value of teamwork. I lost twenty pounds during hell week, which was the worst part of football camp. TORTURE. Hell week included double trainings each day, starting at seven a.m. with a break from eleven to one, and then back at it until six or seven p.m. We were really pushed at this time to see who had what it took to earn a position on the team. Football also greatly helped continue to build my confidence. It gave me the opportunity to work in a team environment where you could make no excuses. I felt like I was part of a select group. All in all, sports were a critical part of my maturity going into high school and I would recommend joining any kind of sport or group in school if possible.

My new self-assurance was soon to be tested.

In auto shop class one day after football season, I witnessed a group of older classmates picking on an overweight and kind of a nerdy kid. It really bothered me to watch because *I* was that kid once. The teacher didn't seem to care much and allowed it to continue. I finally had seen enough and told them to just leave the boy alone. I'd never stuck up for anyone else before and didn't truly understand the repercussions of my actions. It just felt right to say something. Annoyed at being called out, the three bullies switched their focus to me. Everyone heard their boastful promise to get me after school.

Here we go again. But this time I wasn't about to let kids take advantage of me. All those years of pent-up anger from being jumped and being picked on came to a head. As I exited the auto shop classroom I was shoved against a fence and surrounded by a group of hyped-up kids. But it was different this time. I wasn't going to be jumped by a gang—only the ringleader bully, who happened to be several grades older than me. He called me out and then put his fists up to signal it was time to fight.

This time I didn't plead or hesitate. I kicked him right in the stomach. He slouched over and I followed up with several punches. I grabbed him by the hair and slammed his stunned face into the fence before continuing to punch him. His friends eventually pulled me off, then scurried away.

An unbelievable feeling came over me that I can't even describe. All the years of being beat up and picked on were now over in an instant. I came out unscathed and triumphant. Admittedly, we both got in big trouble for that fight, yet all kids could talk about was how a freshman beat up a junior outside auto shop class. I am not condoning violence, but I was cornered and felt I had no choice. No one should be picked on and made fun of; we are all equals. You must stand up for yourself. Thankfully, having good friends, martial arts, and sports gave me the confidence to stand up for myself. It was a pivotal point in my maturity and growth as a young person.

And I was not messed with again after earning my stripes at that school.

CHAPTER FOUR

OPPORTUNITY KNOCKS AGAIN

T HAT FIRST YEAR in high school, a friend asked if I wanted some soda. Of course I did, and we began to drink it. He then told me he had tons more and we could drink it forever. I asked him where it all came from and he said from family, but I did not entirely believe his good fortune. I had a funny feeling about it. I asked him to take me to the stash of soda, so he did. He was right—there was a ton of it. I'd guess at least twenty cases. Still not believing how it was obtained but not really caring, I said, "I think I know how we can make some money . . . if you're interested in bringing me in on it." He agreed.

If we sold it for a little less than everyone else—like fifty or twenty-five cents per can—we could make some quick money. He liked the idea but was not sure *where* to sell it.

"How about school?" I said. "We could bring in backpacks full of different soda and sell it from our lockers. What do you think?"

He loved the idea and we were in business. I did not realize it at the time, but I was pretty good at making something out of nothing and selling in general.

We successfully sold soda out of our lockers for about two weeks until we finally ran out of product. I thought I was in decent shape until another friend's mother overheard me talking to her son about how I made all this money selling soda in my locker. She grilled me, and because I refused to tell her which friend I was selling with, she told my mother and I was forced to take the punishment on my own. I had a feeling that my business partner did not truthfully get the soda from his family, but he would not tell me differently, and I did not press the issue. Now confronted, I took the hit and lost all my money.

I made a poor decision by selling soda from my locker at school, but I really wanted to make some needed money. I learned a valuable lesson that day about the risk associated with breaking rules. In my heart I knew what I was doing was wrong and paid the price.

BONUS POINT: Working hard at a young age is admirable and will build a good foundation for success when you grow up. But you should always follow the rules and trust your gut instinct, regardless of how much you want something.

Soon after the "soda incident," things deteriorated with both my living situation and my mother's finances. My mother separated from Dave and made the very difficult decision to pull me out of school, pack what little belongings we had, and move us eight hundred miles away to live with her friends in southern Oregon. This was very difficult at the time, but was an absolute necessity, as we had nowhere to go in Southern California.

I can remember all my California friends making fun of me for moving to a small town. They joked about me being jumped by farmers with corn husks. But this was going to be my new life and I had to make the best of it.

We moved in with George and Taffy, who shared a small, two-bedroom home with one baby and another on the way. To say we were in tight quarters was an understatement. Taffy and George were kind and wonderful people to invite us to their home. George tirelessly worked full-time installing countertops while building bookcases on the weekends to make ends meet. He was a great provider for his family. My favorite night was Friday night because George always bought everybody pizza, and it was very rare living in Southern California that I ate pizza.

I JUST GOT HERE AND I'M BEING PICKED ON AGAIN?

While playing basketball in the gym on my first day of school, I was confronted by a boy who was making fun of me because I was the new kid from California. He kept calling me "the California boy"—which, as far as insults go, is really dumb. I ignored it at first, but then the boy threw a basketball at me and his comments got more aggressive. I asked him to leave me alone and then he pushed me.

After my experience in auto shop with the bullies a few months prior, I knew I could take care of my business, so I did and that was the end of that. I was never again picked on for being from California or anything else for that matter. One thing I learned to appreciate about southern Oregon was that when two people had an issue they solved it one-on-one versus many-on-one, like when I was jumped by gangs. Again, I'm not *condoning* fighting, but if you must fight, one-on-one is the preferred method, believe me.

GOOD FRIENDS ARE SO IMPORTANT

Our host George had a younger brother, Ricky, who was just three years older than me. Ricky ran around with several other eighteen year olds. I had just turned fifteen, so I thought it was cool to get to hang out with older kids. I hung with a lot of Ricky's friends while attending school and reached a point where they were more my friends than his. I remember when one guy named Travis invited me to a party and I told him that Ricky didn't invite me. "Who cares if Ricky comes or not," Travis said. "You're cool with us and you're invited."

I honestly looked up to Ricky but there were several instances when his true colors would come out. He would get angry if I played better basketball or football or anything for that matter than him. At times he would make me feel like I was not wanted or was a loser. He would push me away. I did not understand his behavior and had no one to talk to about it until Travis came along. I found out later this was just Ricky's own insecurity.

As I developed a deeper friendship with Travis, I began to see what a true friend was like. I asked Travis one day, "Why do you even like me? Why would you invite me to parties over Ricky, and hang out with me on the basketball court?"

He replied, "You've done nothing wrong. You just want to hang out and you're honest and real. Hang out with us anytime."

From that day forward, Travis would not only be one of my best friends but he would also open my eyes to the value of watching out for each other on every level, and what it takes to build that mutual respect that I knew nothing about.

Eventually, my mother managed to get a run-down, two-bedroom apartment on the southside of town. It wasn't great but all she could afford, and it was *ours*. I loved having our own place, even if the apartment had rats that would eat big holes through our walls. We lived there for about six months before my mother got to a point where she couldn't stand living in southern Oregon anymore. She missed her friends and family and made the decision to go back down to California. At this point I had developed a sense of independence—maybe because I had some older friends or perhaps because I thought I could do better. I really do not know, but I was not going back. I had a discussion with my mother and told her I didn't want to go back to the gang-infested, dangerous, horrible place we left behind. I asked her if there was any way I could stay. She had a conversation with George and Taffy and they welcomed me back in.

My mother was given a 1965 Mustang by my father as payment for back debt he owed her and my mother's plan was always to give it to me when I was of age. She left this car and its keys with George and Taffy with instructions to give it to me when I got my license. With only months to go before turning sixteen, I had that car to look forward to.

For a short time, this arrangement worked and I could remain in southern Oregon.

ALL GOOD THINGS MUST COME TO AN END

Unfortunately, soon after my mom went back to Southern California, George and Taffy separated. George moved into a one-bedroom trailer and, with money really tight for Taffy, I had no choice but to move in with him. The small trailer was dingy and outside my school district. I was thankful to George for giving me a temporary place to crash, but the tight quarters felt like an imposition. I made a major decision to chart my own course. Once made, I took the keys to the Mustang, left the trailer behind, and never looked back.

I was officially on my own at the age of fifteen.

CHAPTER FIVE

THE FAST PATH TO ADULTHOOD

OVER THE NEXT YEAR, many things happened. I accidentally totaled the Mustang by rolling it off a mountainside (this can happen when you've never had a driver's license), acquired a work permit, and got a part-time job at a fast-food restaurant. I lived on various friends' couches and sometimes slept in parks and rest stops. I worked hard at figuring out life while still managing to go to school.

From the ages of fifteen to sixteen, I truly had to develop independence and a system of survival. I knew I had to keep moving, working, and hustling to make it. It was not easy convincing people to give me a place to stay or a job opportunity, but as I met new friends I honed my people skills and it became a bit easier.

You might ask where my mother was at this point. Well, she was continuing to struggle in Southern California and would eventually find her way back up, but that's well after I'd been on my own.

It was so important for me at the time to get close to the people in my circle of influence. I had few friends, so I really looked up to people like Travis as an inspiration. He was older, popular, and could play several sports well. I was thankful he was my friend. He may never know how important he was to me back then, but he changed my life for the better and really helped me through some of the toughest times on my own.

Even while struggling with adult responsibilities, I was still a teenager. I wanted nothing more than to go out and socialize at dance clubs and parties. While living with a friend at a trailer park, I would put on a backpack and walk up to twelve miles several times per week just to go to the dance club to hang out—even if I went alone. I did this because it was the only place where I felt like I fit in—a place where I could be whoever I wanted to be. It was also one of the few places where I felt my status was elevated, or like I led a "normal life." Listening to all the great music and dancing for hours with girls made me feel important. It made me feel like I could do *anything*. I drew energy from all the gathered people. If those girls saw where I lived, they may not have even talked to me. But there I felt free. Back then, dancing and basketball were the only things I was good at, so I participated whenever I could. Time spent there certainly made a difference in my life for the better.

Having so little, I created this facade of sorts by often borrowing clothes from friends. Sometimes they didn't even fit, but they made me feel important because they were nicer than mine. My buddies and I would dress up to go to the clubs and dance the night away. People instinctively wanted to hang out with my group of friends and I could not understand why. We were all basically broke young people on our own who barely had enough to pay a five-dollar cover charge, but I guess we looked the part with our borrowed clothes, dancing skills, street smarts, and effortless gift of gab.

Everyone wants to be loved and accepted and to feel relevant, so I had to create what I thought would fill the void. I would find out later in life that money, status, and nice clothes mean nothing, but at the time it was a necessity for me to get through. I lost myself in that world to cope with mine. Socializing definitely built up my confidence and people skills at an early age, but I did not realize until later that that's what I was doing.

I can say today that several of us from that original group are now accomplished sales and business professionals doing amazing things. I guess all that facade stuff and clubbing paid off. Who would have thought?

I did what I had to do to deal with my challenges.

BONUS POINT: Everyone must find their own nondestructive way of dealing with their feelings and find something they can draw strength and hope from. It's really hard to know how to cope when you're struggling at a young age, so you will need to step up, look outside yourself, and make a change. One way might be to lose yourself in a sport or a hobby. Another may be to read books at an early age. If going to school is not an option then find a way to educate yourself. Maybe a commitment to religion. You could try selecting different friends to hang out with, or surround yourself with positive influences. Try something that you're not sure you can do and challenge yourself until you accomplish it. It could change your life or build your confidence to a level you never thought possible. If you must, change your environment. Moving around most of my life was a challenge and scary, but it may have actually helped me develop better people skills. I always had to make new friends and find a way to fit in.

The reality about being young is that almost everything in your life will change or evolve by adulthood. Your environment will likely change. Your friends—at least most of them—will certainly change. And most likely your circumstances will too. So, work at changing it for the positive and don't worry about the small stuff in your head.

At the age of sixteen, I worked my way into a position at a juice store in the mall, which was a welcome pay increase from fast food. From there I developed relationships with several stores, including one called America the Beautiful Dreamer that sold futons. There I was offered a part-time position cleaning, setting up, and assisting sales associates when they needed it. I wore a tie for the first time and felt like a professional. I was really proud of that job. Lodging-wise, after living on couches and being homeless for a brief period, I was offered a room from a nice young couple through a mutual friend. They even lived in an apartment across the street from the mall where I worked. In one year's time of being on my own, I had worked my way into living in a nice apartment, wearing business clothes, and learning how to support myself.

In my limited free time I would hang out with a diverse group at a minors dance club called REMIX. I went there every week to unwind, dance, meet girls, and make new friends. I was told I was a good dancer and this made it easy to fit in, but going to that club did not come without its risks. One time I was wearing some Cross Colours clothing (cool club clothes for the time) and two guys approached me right outside the club. They asked me who I thought I was. I did not quite understand what the issue was, but they were unrelenting in their pestering. They began to get a bit more aggressive and one of them got right up in my face. These two guys were much bigger than me and I thought for sure I was going to get jumped.

Out of nowhere, one of the guys gets punched in the head so hard he literally flipped over the railing and was out cold in the street. His friend who was in my face ran off. I looked up and recognized Bob, a larger than life rugged outdoors type of guy, whose hands were twice the width of mine and had been in more fights than anyone I had heard of in the entire town. Bob was as tough as they come. I had barely said a few words to him before that night, but he approached and asked, "Are you okay? Anyone that hangs with my little brother is like my little brother and those guys are out-of-town punks. You let me know if you ever need anything. I've got your back."

Wow, I could not believe it. Someone stood up for me, and I did nothing to deserve it other than be a good friend to his little brother. Bob walked back in the club as if nothing had happened.

Just when I thought I was building my life, things became a bit challenging when the couple I was living with split up. I was forced to move out and away from the mall. I didn't have a car, so my only option was to quit the futon store job and stay with friends for the next year. I went to school and worked odd jobs. At one point I had no place to go and a friend's mother offered their garage behind the house. It wasn't much of an apartment, but it had a bed and a refrigerator, and they just asked that I contribute to the power bill. I lived in this garage for about nine months. *Cool,* I thought, *I'm seventeen years old and I've got my very own garage apartment.*

I'm not going to lie—it was really cold, lonely, and a bit scary in the garage. While living there I really had to hustle for everything; working part-time just didn't cut it being on my own. After moving on from the garage, I scrounged for cans and hustled for extra money and slept again on couches and at parks. When you're on your own at that age, there are not many options. I enrolled back in school for a brief period and really tried hard, but working *and* going to school just wasn't an available option for me. It was one or the other. I dropped out again and continued working a *second* job to support myself.

During this period from the age of sixteen to about eighteen, I was in many fights, most of which were standing my ground and defending myself. I won them all. Most of the altercations occurred while couch surfing from one place to the next. I crossed paths with some shady kids in these situations and had no choice but to fight to win. Thankfully, I had lots of training and street smarts that can only be developed while surviving on your own. Fighting at that age and in that environment was more about building a reputation. You were either a lion or a gazelle, and there were lots of egos.

Most of the younger people in town went cruising around the city on weekend nights, stopping at specific spots and hanging out. It was just something to do and a common way for people to show off their cool rides. One night I was with two friends, riding in a white Acura with expensive gold Dayton wire wheels on it. We stopped at a light in front of the REMIX dance club, pulling up next to a Monte Carlo. I noticed that its four occupants did not look local. It was a common occurrence for thugs to come up from northern California for the weekend and party in our town. Someone in the Monte Carlo yelled to us: "Hey, homey, nice wheels. Why don't you give them up?" A few choice words were exchanged between my friend who was driving and the passenger of the Monte Carlo. The light turned green and they sped away. And then things escalated.

A little later, after meeting up with another friend and sharing the prior confrontation, we decided to track down this Monte Carlo.

As we drove through town on cruising night, we eventually spotted the Monte Carlo at about one a.m. heading toward Main Street. My two friends with the Acura, followed by me and another friend driving a Honda Civic, pulled behind the Monte Carlo at a stoplight. I distinctly remember it being a cold, foggy night. Just as my friend on the passenger side of the Acura leaned out and started yelling something at the Monte Carlo's passengers, shots rang out. Someone on the passenger side of the Monte Carlo was leaning out the window and shooting at both our cars! My side of the windshield splintered. I could not believe what I was seeing. Immediately I ducked below the dashboard as bullets hit both of my friends' cars several times and glass flew everywhere. I kept thinking, *Oh my god, they are going to kill us.* And then the gunfire stopped and I heard screeching wheels. Remarkably, everyone was okay and we got out of there as quick as we could.

We were very lucky. One of us could have lost our lives that day for *car rims.* Thankfully the police caught everyone involved. A few years later, the sister of the shooter worked for me and I found out that after being convicted for his crimes, her brother was released from jail only to fatally stab another man and go to prison for another twenty years. I still have the original newspaper clipping about the shooting as a reminder of how precious life is. Life is made up of many moments—remember to create positive moments and avoid the negative ones. It's not always worth it to save face. Sometimes, you just need to walk away.

I once lost a fight and deserved it. I had a disagreement with a friend who was much bigger than me and—to be honest—he was in the right. Stupidly, I escalated the disagreement and went to his house late one evening to confront him. We settled the argument, but then I looked away for a split second and he knocked me out cold. He really beat me up good, even dragging me through a blackberry bush afterward for a final kick to the face. I truly looked like a monster the next day, between the cuts and bruises and having to pull thorns out of my face. That was the first and last time in my life I lost a one-on-one fight. I learned from it and was humbled. When you're wrong, admit it, and work to find a reasonable solution.

Things got so bad at one point that I was living with three other friends in a one-bedroom trailer outside town. I remember only one of us was working full-time and he carried the load while the rest of us worked odd jobs, collected cans to turn in for cash, or did whatever we could for extra money. And because I was living so far outside town, I was forced once again to drop out of school. After a while I realized my life was going nowhere.

Now that I was an adult, I made the decision to reach out to my dad. He was not much of a part of my life growing up, but I thought this might be an opportunity for me to develop a relationship. He too had a hard life, just like my mother, and I still loved them both regardless of the way things were. He offered me the opportunity to come down to stay with him and his mother in California. He said maybe he could show me where to go get a job and build a life. Reluctantly I went back down to California, but I really didn't have a choice. I slept on the sofa in my dad's living room and clearly remember the grandfather clock chiming and how lonely I felt being there. Of course, I was very thankful and planned to earn my keep, but it was a hard reality.

Within a week, my dad sent me to apply at an auto parts warehouse stocking product. He told me that if I saved up enough money he would sell me his used 1982 Chevy pickup. I worked hard in that warehouse—eventually earning about $380. My father told me that he appreciated my hard work, so he sold me the Chevy for the $380. It was all my money, but I earned it and was buying my own truck with it. Afterward, I called a few friends in Oregon and asked if anybody had a place I could stay now that I had a vehicle. I could find a full-time job and pay my own way. My dad and I never really had a tight relationship, but I don't blame him for that.

I settled back in southern Oregon, living on the sofa at a friend's apartment. I soon found a job working part-time in a furniture store warehouse. I got this job through a friend that I met while playing basketball at the YMCA. His name was Tony.

I played basketball as much as I could—sometimes for five hours at a time. Tony approached me on the court one night after my group had run with no losses. "Hey man, you're good," he said. "I was wondering if you would mind teaching me a few things?" He was new in town and really wanted to learn. Without hesitation, I agreed, and we have been friends for twenty-plus years. Basketball and selflessness are what connected our friendship.

The point I'm making is that it's okay to lend a helping hand and take time out of your day to make a difference or show someone you care. It feels good and could make a significant difference in someone's life. I can tell you from experience that our friendship helped us both through some tough times—plus it led to a needed job opportunity, as Tony was the manager of the store.

In a brief period, I had picked up so much of the workload that I went from sweeping the warehouse and cleaning, to warehouse work, to eventually becoming the warehouse manager. I was told I worked so fast and efficiently that the other warehouse person was let go and I handled all the duties on my own, including loading the delivery truck. I was not given much in life that I had not earned, and I really felt this job was an opportunity for me to start a career. I worked hard for this store, proving myself worthy of the position.

After about six months, Tony told me that the owner would soon give me a raise of approximately $400 a month, taking me to $1,600. This was a big deal because at $1,600, I could get my own place. I was thrilled, but what I *really* wanted to try was selling. The furniture store ran a noncommissioned format, so I asked Tony one day if I could take a break from the warehouse and go on to the store floor to sell furniture. Tony asked the owner, who said no. When I questioned why I couldn't have the opportunity to sell, Tony said that he thought it had to do with money.

"Tell the owner I'm willing to work for free on a weekend," I said. "I just want to see if I can sell."

The owner agreed to let me work that weekend for free and I don't think he regretted it, as my efforts resulted in *half* the store's sales that day, and there were four salespeople.

I will never forget my first sale. It was a $4,000 leather set that had just come in from a new vendor. The owner was ecstatic. When the dust settled I asked Tony if now there was an opportunity for me to go to the sales floor full-time. He came back and regrettably said no. They had too many salespeople on the floor already and the decision came directly from the owner. I thought to myself, *The salespeople don't even make commission and I outsold them. Why wouldn't I be given a chance to sell?* Tony, being my friend as much as manager, confided, "I really think it's money. It's possibly about maturity, but likely money more than anything else."

A few months went by and I asked about my promised raise for doing such a fine job at the warehouse. Tony met with the owner and then returned with a surprise.

"The owner knows you want to be on the sales floor," Tony said, "but he really doesn't want you to leave. He also doesn't want to give you a raise just to try to keep you here, so he's going to give you those barstools that you liked as a bonus if you hang in there a little bit longer. Later he'll revisit that raise."

That was the first time I truly learned that things are not always what they seem, and you're not guaranteed anything in life. The disappointment really hurt my feelings. I had worked so hard in that warehouse and sold so much better than those actual sales associates, and yet I was passed by as though I added no value to the organization. My friend tried to talk me down and told me to hang in there, but I had had enough. It was clear, regardless of my maturity, that the owner didn't respect me or the hard work ethic that I had brought to the organization. So, I moved on. Come on . . . all that demonstrated hard work for a few discontinued barstools? No thanks.

BONUS POINT: It's not always going to work out the way you want it to, but you need to work really hard no matter what. Don't take it personally or be angry. Instead, use the energy to drive yourself forward to the next opportunity, as there is *always* a next opportunity. If you are not being valued for proven work, then move on.

A HOTDOG CART BECOMES AN UNLIKELY SUCCESS STORY

As I tried to figure out what to do next, I took a part-time gig at a department store. While working there I met a girl named Michele who worked at a hardware store, and eventually I moved in with her. The hardware store is relevant because when I would go to visit her, I would always say hi to the hotdog cart guy out front whose name was Mike. As I got to know Mike over the next year I learned that hotdog cart guys make pretty good money and have lots of freedom. He told me of an opportunity that was coming up with the other cart in front of the G.I. Joe's department store and could put in a good word if I was interested. He also told me that I would start at about $1,600 a month plus tips. I thought to myself, *Is he crazy? I can make $1,600 a month plus tips running a hotdog cart?* I interviewed with the owner and was soon hired to run my own hotdog cart after Mike's recommendation.

For the first year I ran the cart, many friends made fun of me for working there, but I made more money and had more freedom than all of them. I also began to learn what it took to own and run a business. None of my friends were doing that, and when we went out, *I* was the one who always had money.

I learned a lot while working at that cart—specifically how to deal with other people. The owner of the carts, Al, would come by and check to make sure you were working and your attitude was good with the customers. He taught me plenty about the basics of human nature and selling.

Al was the first real mentor in my life and I'm forever grateful that we crossed paths. It was an excellent job experience that I do not regret for one minute.

And it ultimately led to much bigger things.

CHAPTER SIX

THE JOB THAT CHANGED EVERYTHING

M Y GIRLFRIEND and I broke up and I moved in with Mike. That went on for about nine months until I woke up one night and found that Mike had taken the VCR and the computer completely apart and spread out about five hundred parts all over the living room floor. I was familiar with drugs and addiction because I had seen this devastating disease before in others.

I was exposed to drugs many times before the age of eighteen. They always seemed to be around at parties or in circles of friends. Thankfully, my mother had a strong influence on my choice to stay away from them. I saw firsthand how alcohol and drugs can ruin and sometimes end people's lives. Alcohol and drugs impair judgment and can cause people to lose focus on what's important. Eventually my stepfather committed suicide because of his addiction. I really hated drugs, and as I grew older, I hated them even more. I developed a sense of fear that if I ever tried them even once that I might lose control. If that happened I could lose everything in my life, and that scared the hell out of me. I did not have much, but to this day that fear is still there and has always kept me away from them.

Drugs of all kinds are very destructive and can take time to show their effects. Most people will not have the luxury of seeing what drugs are capable of and I'm glad I *did* because it has always kept me away, even when people made fun of me because I would not partake. I say "luxury" because to truly appreciate the devastation one may need to witness it. I confronted Mike and found out that he was addicted to methamphetamine and pain pills.

On top of dealing with my crazy, drug-using roommate, my father's former Chevy was completely broken down in the driveway. As its replacement, I bought a Mazda RX7 that literally had to be pushed backward in order to get it to start, almost every time. I paid way too much for that lemon that never worked right.

It was time for me to move on. I had nowhere else to go, but my luck was about to change.

One Saturday afternoon I had a line of about twenty people at my hotdog cart. It was a beautiful day, the tips were good, and I was in the zone. I generally had a good attitude because I always thought about where I'd come from and how many challenges I had growing up. I was very thankful to be working and have the freedom I had working that hotdog cart.

That day I was plugging along, joking with the customers, when two men approached me after the line died down. One man, who introduced himself as Ron, said to me, "You know, you have a good attitude. I've been watching you every weekend for the last three weeks. I come by and get a hotdog and you're always in a good mood and take care of the customers. I need a guy like you on my team."

The first thing that came to my mind was, *Great. This is one of those telemarketing, door-to-door deals, or one of those pyramid schemes.*

"Are you familiar with the construction going on in Central Point, just north of here?" he asked.

I said no.

Then he told me he was building the largest family fun center within four hundred miles, and introduced me to his general manager. He repeated that he really wanted a guy like me on his team.

I asked him what he had in mind.

Ron said he had many positions to fill and could start me as a ride manager and I could work my way up to a supervisor.

I told him I was happy where I was and if I was going to leave it would have to be a step up.

He asked what I wanted.

"Well, I would like a starting supervisor position and medical benefits," I said. I told him that he would get more out of me than he paid for, and that I was willing to work as many hours as it takes, and would do anything to help the business.

"I tell you what," he replied, "let me discuss this with my general manager and I'll get back to you next week."

I didn't give much more thought to it, but the very next day Ron came back and offered me a $1,600 salary a month, a starting supervisor position, *and* medical benefits. I could not believe it. I just earned the position of my life and didn't even have to apply for it.

I didn't know it at the time, but this job and Ron would completely change my personal and professional life forever.

I called my mother to tell her the incredible news. I found a four-bedroom house on Main Street in a nice neighborhood and then asked my mom if she and my grandmother would like to move in and share the house with me. It didn't take long for my mother, my grandmother, and my cousin to all leave California and move in with me in this beautiful home. Life was going pretty well. I had a great house on the hill, my family was with me, and I landed a new job at the hottest new business in the valley. I was on cloud nine and starting to feel like a responsible adult.

BONUS POINT: Don't be afraid to ask for what you want—especially if someone is trying to solicit you from another business. You have value and the person on the other side may be underestimating what that value is. If you ask a potential employer for something, be ready to offer something in return. Don't blow smoke just to get a job or better pay. You'd better deliver if you make a bold statement. Your reputation is very important and you may not get another chance to prove your worth. Life is not all about money and status. I have turned down positions offering just that— higher pay or status—but did not transition to those opportunities because *my* priorities and principles did not align with the opportunities.

Working with Ron at the Rogue Valley Family Fun Center began to sculpt my adult personality, teaching me lifelong problem-solving skills while helping me to build a stronger work ethic that would serve me the rest of my life. Ron was a no-nonsense, get your hands dirty kind of person. He had a wonderful family: a loving wife, Margie, and two wonderful kids, who were never far from his side. I don't know that Ron will ever truly understand how much of an influence he had on me, but he did. I had read a few books at this point in my life, but Ron took the value of reading to a whole other level and was the most influential mentor I ever met.

Ron introduced me and the other managers to the book *How to Win Friends and Influence People* by Dale Carnegie. He not only introduced this book to us, but he made us read chapters and discuss them every few weeks. I was the only manager of the three who read the book religiously. I found so much value in the book's content and how Ron related the chapters to our everyday management of the business. Ron truly had a way of bridging the gap between knowledge and applying that knowledge to your advantage. He had retired wealthy at the age of forty-four from his CPA firm and decided to open the Fun Center because he loved kids. Plus I imagine he just could not bear to think of simply golfing and fishing for the next forty years. I was inspired by this because he didn't *need* the Fun Center; he did it because he loved being an entrepreneur.

Ron had multiple streams of income. He was a managing partner in a water park in Southern California, had sold his CPA firm for a nice profit, and had multiple rental properties. Ron was a true entrepreneur and was extremely passionate about building businesses and solving problems.

TOUGH LESSONS LEARNED

While the Fun Center was being constructed Ron gave us the opportunity to put in as many hours as we wanted, which gave me the opportunity to make extra money. You learn a lot about business when you're building a Fun Center from the ground up. A few of the early responsibilities I had were to develop a training and procedure manual for the go-kart track, manage the boat pond, and supervise the chlorination process. I developed a good training manual and was praised by Ron for my efforts.

The boat pond was another story.

While managing the chlorinator, I messed up my calculations, completely destroying the seals on the boat pond after running it for only six months. This over-chlorination caused the clear coat to deteriorate and ultimately ruin the bottom of the pond. This rookie mistake cost Ron approximately $10,000, but as usual, Ron used it as a teaching opportunity. He went through the entire process, held me accountable, and worked me through viable solutions going forward. I can't tell you how constructive this process was. I was still a young person trying to understand a very complicated world, but Ron knew that. He was very good at minimizing problems and magnifying solutions. He always made me feel as though I would get through anything and be stronger on the other side.

Ron gave many of his employees the additional opportunity to come out to work on his personal property before and after work to make extra money. I remember he asked if anyone would like to help put in order what would eventually become a guest house but for now was his primary residence. They had to prepare it to live in while they built their custom home below on the lower part of the property. I did not hesitate to say yes and showed up at his house at seven a.m. even though I had to work later that afternoon at the Fun Center. When I got there Ron asked, "Have you ever worked on sewage lines?"

"I haven't really worked on anything," I admitted.

He laughed. "Well then, we will learn together."

This was the first lesson Ron taught me about solving your own problems. He had a way of looking at problems as opportunities not only to teach, but to save time and money. As I worked with Ron for the next few years, I realized it wasn't about money with Ron; it was about the challenge and finding solutions.

There were several weeks one summer while working at Ron's house that I put in a combined one-hundred-hour work week. Some days I would get up at six a.m. to start work at Ron's until my shift at two p.m. started at the Fun Center, and then work there till ten p.m. And I worked many weeks seven days a week. Ron said he would pay me as long as I wanted to work and I took full advantage of that—more so than anyone else in the entire organization that had the same offer. It was great to make all the extra money, but I gained far more by working closely with Ron every day. I loved it. In a sense, he was like a father figure to me, and I could not get enough of his time.

While working with Ron on his property I learned how to do basic plumbing, electric, tree trimming, landscaping, and much more. We also worked a lot on problem-solving. He would say things like: "What would you do if I were not here?", or "How would you solve this problem?" This was so important in developing my independence as a business person later in life.

BONUS POINT: There are mentors all around us. You just have to be open to them sharing their wisdom. Ask lots of questions and work hard for them. Volunteer, work for free, and do whatever it takes to get time with them. You will not know till later in life how important this is, but I'm telling you it could be the *single most important thing in your life*, and if you're not paying attention, you will miss it.

The Fun Center originally had a general manager, an assistant manager, and three park supervisors. I was one of the supervisors. After a while Ron made the call to eliminate the positions above supervisor and let the three of us in the lower position lead the park as a team, with one of us as lead. A man named Rod was chosen to lead. He had military experience and was an overall great leader. Rod moved on after a while and Ron promoted me to the lead supervisor (or general manager) of the Fun Center. I really appreciated the opportunity to lead and be in charge.

This only lasted about two weeks.

Unfortunately, I made a bad decision and was demoted back to my original position. I was feeling sick one Saturday, which is a really busy day at the park. I went home after only a few hours into my shift and put someone else in charge. I was available for calls, but really felt I needed to get home and rest.

I made a bad judgment call. I did not notify the owner because I felt that he would be bothered, and I thought I was covering my bases. Ron was right in demoting me, because at the time what I thought was a good decision could have put the park in jeopardy and I should have notified him. I was clearly not ready to lead a multimillion-dollar organization at the age of nineteen.

The takeaway here is, it's okay to take criticism and fail. There are more lessons learned in most cases failing than in successful ones.

A BRUSH WITH DANGER

One day while managing, all Ron's mentoring paid off in a big way. While watching the go-kart track from the second level office, I noticed one of the employees letting riders on the track for free. I was not 100 percent sure because I could not see the transaction, but had reason enough to investigate further. I waited until the employee went on break and audited the tickets and ride count and found a big discrepancy during his shift. I then confronted the employee and he tried to explain it away. I had the sense he knew he was caught, yet I told him it was not anything to worry about. I just had to ask.

Later that evening, I was confronted at the bottom of the stairs to the manager's office by a friend of the employee I confronted earlier, who was also an employee. This employee began to raise his voice as he accused me of starting trouble. He stated that his friend had done nothing wrong and said I had better stop making things up. This employee had been rumored to be taking steroids, as well as possibly distributing those drugs. I was not quite sure what he was capable of, but I was about to find out.

To try to calm things down I asked if he would mind joining me in the manager's office to finish our discussion. As soon as we got there and the door closed, he became enraged. This employee outweighed me by about forty pounds and was very muscular. He had a wild look in his eyes that I'd never seen before. He was so angry and was yelling so loudly I knew something wasn't quite right. I tried to reason with him—telling him that I simply questioned his friend and I could not discuss the details of our conversation. But this just enraged him further.

"If you take this any further, I will kill you," he said. "If you don't believe me, try me. I have nothing to lose."

Now I had been in many challenging situations in my life before this incident and thought I was mentally prepared for pretty much anything, but when someone threatens they're going to *kill you*, and they have the physical strength and the mentality to do it, a certain fear comes over you that you can't quite explain until you experience it. By some way of a miracle, something snapped him back to reality, and he left the office. But not before slamming the door after yelling profanities.

After the incident I called Ron and explained the situation. He asked if I wanted to go home but I said no. I *was* a bit shaken but wanted to stay and finish my shift. The next day Ron and all the supervisors gathered to discuss how we would deal with these employees. It was decided that another supervisor would terminate both employees at separate times a week or so later. While they would know why they were being fired collectively, we thought it would be best to let some time pass, hopefully cooling down the situation.

I was really struck some years later when I heard that this angry individual was incarcerated for trafficking steroids and later being part of a group that beat a man to death. The deceased had apparently been part of their group and was being punished for stealing their stash. It's amazing how small moments in your life have the potential to make such a big difference. Had I not been taught to control my emotions and how to deal with potential employee issues after several years of Ron's mentoring, things may have turned out differently. That lesson in managing people always stuck with me, and for good reason, because you never know who you're dealing with and what their motivations might be.

BONUS POINT: Always treat people with respect, and remember, you're seeing things from your frame of reference and not theirs.

As time passed, I continued to learn and evolve until, at age twenty, I had a conversation with Ron about my future at the Fun Center. I was getting a bit impatient and really wanted to move to the next level. Ron and I talked in general about life and work for some time. Just before the conversation ended, Ron turned to me and said, "You know, Chris, I've watched you work this Fun Center for several years and I've seen you grow and mature. I would love to have you here forever, but I really think you're missing a calling. With your personality, I really think you should be selling. You'd be a great salesperson and I feel like you're not utilizing what you're best at working at the Fun Center."

At the time, even though I had sold a little bit, I really thought he was crazy. Of course, I say that in a lighthearted manner. The truth was I really felt at home at the Fun Center and thought I would work there forever. But Ron was my mentor and I took his advice very seriously. I wouldn't know it at the time, but his comments that day would change the course of my life and lead me to the success and effectiveness that I now have in my professional life.

CHAPTER SEVEN

A NEW BEGINNING FROM THE MOST UNLIKELY PLACE

I TOOK RON'S ADVICE and took a job with a janitorial products sales company that had been pursuing me for about six months. The owner presented a lucrative opportunity with base pay and commissions. I had not worked in commissions before, but the picture he painted was pretty enticing and an increase in pay from what I was currently making at the Fun Center.

It only took about three months for me to realize that the owner's projections were quite inflated. While I sold new accounts and added services to existing accounts, I barely broke my base each month. This was a bit discouraging. My mentor had said I was missing my calling. How could I *not* be successful selling? But perhaps this just wasn't the field of selling I should be in.

The grass is not always greener on the other side. It's just different grass. Now I don't regret leaving the Fun Center, but at that point in my life I did.

I was twenty-one years old and basically unemployed. For a while I was one of the few in the house working full-time. Those were good times. Now my housemates and I ate primarily potatoes and ramen for dinner. We all helped one another as much as we could, but I felt overwhelmingly defeated. I had thought that I was finally over the hump. I really needed to pull myself out of this hole and get back on track.

BONUS POINT: It's okay to pursue other opportunities and get outside your comfort zone, but be sure you're doing it for the right reasons, and really think through all the potential outcomes before making the final decision to move on.

WHY NOT TO DRIVE ON A SUSPENDED LICENSE

One night I borrowed my grandma's white station wagon to drive my friends around. Technically, I was not supposed to be driving because I had a suspended license from unpaid tickets. But I thought we would be fine, as I was not driving far—just picking up two buddies to all grab a bite to eat. We met a couple girls at the local fast-food place and they wanted to hang out, so we all caravanned back to hang at our place.

My two friends had been drinking, but they were of legal age, and I was driving, so it didn't seem like a big deal. Then, about a mile from my house, one of my drunk friends decides to climb up on the vehicle's hood while I'm driving and crazily "surf." I tried to coax him down and back inside, but to no avail. On one of the side roads a police car was driving away from us and I saw its brake lights come on as we drove past. I told my friend to *get in the car* and then sped up to get us home as quickly as possible.

I'm one last turn and literally fifty feet from my house when I saw a police car turn the corner. Panicked, I pulled up the drive, jumped out, and ran for the house. Seconds later I could hear the police yelling at me but I didn't turn back as I jumped neighboring fences and then hid out in some bushes. I was so scared of getting caught that I stayed hidden for at least one and a half hours as the police unsuccessfully searched nearby.

Eventually the two girls that were trailing us home drove by where I was hiding and yelled my name. I jumped in their car and they drove me to a place to stay. I found out later that my two friends would not give up my name and were taken to jail, cited for public intoxication, even though there were just sitting in a car when arrested.

They were released the next morning with charges dropped.

I turned myself in a day later. My grandma got her car back from the tow yard, and I received a ticket for driving while suspended, in addition to my stupid pride being damaged. In hindsight, I should have never been driving and I should not have run. (Don't ever run from the police no matter what happens.) I just got scared and instinct took over. I made a stupid mistake that cost me more in the end while putting everyone at risk. I share this particular tale because mistakes will be made, but if you can admit when you are wrong and learn from them, you will be okay.

DON'T KNOCK THE HUSTLE

One thing my friends and I were very good at was socializing. In turn, we were very good at throwing parties. I once worked with a friend running a minors' dance club, and we had lots of success at it. I was the head bouncer, which was funny because I'm not big enough to be intimidating, but believe me, I handled my business well. The club we ran was called Platinum Productions, and the two owners we worked with rented halls on the weekends to fill with four to five hundred kids who wanted a place to dance and listen to great music. One of the owners was an incredible DJ from the East Coast who spun the latest and greatest music not even on the West Coast yet, so it was easy to fill our halls. Lots of money was made, good times were had, and it kept young people off the streets and out of trouble.

This sparked an idea.

My friends and I had been to many parties, and had even hosted a few over the years, so I thought, *Maybe I can make a lot more money doing this on a larger scale.*

A major opportunity arrived one night when we were all underemployed and, yes, having a party at our house. I was approached by an older gentleman who is the uncle of one of our partygoers.

"Would you be willing to throw a party for me," he asked.

"What kind of party are you thinking?" I said.

"I don't know. I'd like to do something like what you're throwing, but twenty times larger."

After I stopped laughing I asked, "How and where would you possibly throw a party *twenty times larger* than this?"

He told me he had a fifty-acre property off Highway 140 with several smaller homes on it, a primary residence, volleyball pits, a large pool, and a private bridge with a security gate to access the property.

Huh. I could not believe the potential opportunity this presented. "Well, this is going take quite a bit of organization," I said to the man. "And how much are you looking to make?"

"I don't want to make anything," he said. "I just want to have a huge party at my house and I want you to throw it."

Okay then. How could I refuse?

After organizing personnel, I began strategizing how we would execute this party. My target was Memorial Day weekend—four weeks away. I asked the owner of the property to front some money for the alcohol, flyers, and anything else we might need to set this up. I would collect money at the door and pay them back for any of the money he contributed plus a bonus. He agreed. Travis, who was a very good friend and roommate at the time, helped me organize the event. Together we borrowed some extra cash from contributors and added it to the party funds, as the owner only had so much money to give. Ultimately, we purchased twenty-five cases and four full-size kegs of beer from the local alcohol distributor, figuring this would be plenty to support the estimated attendance.

For promotion, we printed flyers that read: COME JOIN US AT THE RAGE OFF HWY 140—THE TRIBE IS CALLING. The flyer included a picture of a toilet bowl on the side of the road. The intent was to identify the location on what was otherwise a long and dark road in the middle of nowhere. Plus, we thought the toilet would be a funny marker. The flyer's finer details included: Come out to have the time your life; Bring your tents and sleeping bags; We're partying all weekend . . . or something to that effect. We distributed these flyers to every bar and club in Rogue Valley, as well as distribution through friends' networks.

We could not have anticipated just how good and huge this party would be. The first night we ran out of alcohol by about twelve a.m. and that was with an estimated two hundred to two fifty in attendance and people bringing their own stuff. By the second night, the estimated attendance was more than three-fifty to four hundred. We had DJs spinning on the houses' balconies, a bikini contest, a volleyball tournament, and money flowing through the door like you would not believe. The first night, Friday, we started charging only ten dollars per head, yet ended up charging twenty to thirty dollars because we could. The value of getting in was so high due to word of mouth and all the party had to offer, that people did not even argue about the price. This is when I learned about value and what it means when value exceeds price.

At one point I had to have a pair of brawny bouncers escort me back and forth to the front gate on the bridge to collect the money in a large bag because the doorman could not safely hold it all. I had so much money that I had to hide it in a pile under a sleeping bag in my tent.

The police showed up at one point and tried to cross the bridge and enter the gates, but it was private property and until they had probable cause they could not enter. I made an agreement with them that if we made sure no one left drinking and we let them make a quick pass through the party, would they let us continue? They agreed to the terms. And we held up our end of the promise. Over the three days of our celebration, we had zero reportable incidences and no DUIs, which is remarkable because the party had grown so big, so fast, that we had fifty-three-foot tractor-trailer drivers parked outside from more than one hundred miles away saying they heard through the grapevine at the truck stops *this* was the place to be. We filled the two property parking lots and vehicles were lined up along the highway for at least two hundred yards.

This was by far the best party my group had ever organized. When the dust settled after the party was over I had cleared about $1,500, and that was after paying back the host, bouncers, and contributors. Not bad for one party in three days.

HOW IMPORTANT IS CREDIT? *REALLY* IMPORTANT

Most of the people in my life did not have much money and when things were tough the last thing they talked about was money. I usually heard people say: "We don't have money," or "We're broke," but no one ever explained money or how important it and credit were while I was growing up. I can't remember learning a single thing about money in school other than basic math.

Let me digress for a minute. Here is my first disastrous experience with credit.

When I was seventeen, I applied for an Eddie Bauer credit card at the mall after popping in there to just look at stuff. I had no idea what credit was or the process of getting it, but there was an automated kiosk and I filled out the info. Somehow, I was approved for my first credit card with a $300 line of credit. I asked the lady at the counter how it worked, and she said, "You have $300 to spend, so have fun shopping."

I used it all up in about twenty minutes that day. I knew nothing about credit and as a result soon acquired several cards and loans that I could not pay back. Long story short, after three years of very irresponsible shopping, helping friends, and financing things like crazy, I filed for bankruptcy.

So, there I was, at barely twenty years old with terrible credit and a bankruptcy (BK) on my record. I wish *someone* would have warned me about the importance of credit beforehand. There is not a single item purchased back then that is in my life now. In other words, it was a complete waste of time and money and all about instant gratification. I will touch on credit and finances later in the book but I wanted to highlight this crucial point.

Credit is important and should be respected. I recommend learning as much as you can at an early age about credit and money. You can leverage investments using good credit and you can make incredible deals with cash. You also look good to potential partners, employers, and financial institutions when you have these two things aligned.

CHAPTER EIGHT

SOMETHING HAS TO CHANGE— CARVING A SALES CAREER PATH

A T TWENTY-TWO years old, I was throwing parties, working part-time installing stereos, delivering hot tubs, *and* managing a tanning salon one day per week. Yes, all of that. Crazy, right? But I had to do what I could to make ends meet. And I was willing to do almost anything.

I really had no direction. All the advice and guidance Ron had given me, and I was just wasting it. I found myself lost in the shuffle of life, watching some of my friends make something of themselves, while others were failing or dying or going to jail. I had no path to success and was truly missing the guidance I once had from my mentor. Then I thought back to when Ron said I should be selling—as it was my true calling.

A career in selling *had* to be better than all this craziness I was into with all these random jobs.

I decided to give sales another shot.

First, I started applying to several furniture stores in the area and after the first two interviews I had two job offers. Either I was a natural at this interviewing thing or the furniture stores were desperate. Regardless, I definitely had a knack for communicating with people and selling myself.

After the second interview, I was sitting in a parking lot when my old friend Tony—from the store where I once swept floors—called to offer me what would be a *third* offer in two days. He was now managing two stores in Portland, more than 270 miles north of Medford. He insisted the owner give me a shot, so after some negotiating I was on my way to begin a new chapter in Portland. I was given a $2,000 per month base guarantee until I break that with commission—my highest salary to date.

Now remember, I had not formally sold furniture at this point, so there was a learning curve ahead. To demonstrate, I recall my very first customer—a husband and wife asking for a secretary.

"No problem," I said. "She is sitting right over there." I pointed to the counter.

"No," they said, "a *secretary*."

So I called out, "Hey, Bonnie, these customers are asking for you!"

"No, son. A secretary is a small writing desk."

Wow, I felt like an idiot. My friend gave me a shot and I had no clue what I was doing. How on earth could I sell against all these professionals and make a living? I only thought I knew how to sell. But what I *did* know was how to deal with people. As I worked through the selling process, I went back to what had helped me get through the tough times growing up. I thought about what drove me when I was being picked on or trying to negotiate a place to stay or just survive in general through my first twenty-one years. Selling to people is no different from negotiating through the challenges I've experienced my whole life.

BONUS POINT: You must surround yourself with good mentors and positive influencers, they will have a profound impact your life. You are more likely to attract these kinds of mentors and positive influencers if you have a decent work ethic, show initiative to learn, and apply what you're learning.

HONING MY SKILLS ON THE FLOOR

I began asking all the sales reps to tell me everything they knew about their furniture lines. I watched the top writers closely and made diligent notes on what they did and how they did it. I offered to work any day that others called in sick.

I broke down each element of how we were paid and how I could maximize that to make more money with less work: selling multiple pieces in packages and adding on to my ticket, following up with existing customers during sales, and selling furniture protection plans to everyone who bought furniture.

I quickly realized that product knowledge was not nearly as important as the people, or more importantly, *understanding* the people. What I mean by that is if I learned the behaviors of the other sales associates—the good, bad and ugly—and if I learned more about the customers and what drives them to buy, then all that was left was for me to outwork those around me and utilize my people skills. This is not that hard considering most of selling is talking.

Much of the selling process was about *filling a need* for a consumer or *exposing a pain point* in their life. For example, protection plans. At one point I became so good at selling this program that other sales associates split their commission with me to help close their deals. When I was working a sale, especially in the beginning, I simply made friends with the customers. I'd make light of things in a genuine way, asking them lots of questions like: "Why are you looking for new furniture?" or "What don't you like about what you have?" I would talk a lot about my life and experiences and ask them about theirs. From their reply, I would identify elements of their life that would make them perfect candidates for my protection plan—reasons why this product may enhance their lives, make things easy for them, and give them peace of mind.

Let me give you an example.

A potential client does not want to just hand over $150 to buy air, especially when you call that air a "warranty" and promise them that everything will be great when they use it. *Just go home, Mr. and Mrs. Customer, with this $150 piece of paper (aka, "air") and all your worries will dissolve.*

What?

Instead, I would focus on all the *reasons* they were in the market for a new product and go from there. When you understand someone, it's easier for them to understand you, as Stephen Covey stated in *The Seven Habits of Highly Effective People* (one of my favorite books of all time).

Potential clients understand that it's frustrating to spill something on their sofa and stain it. They understand that when they call an out-of-warranty technician to fix something and pay $89 per hour for it, they'll get frustrated. Clients know that they will eventually damage or stain the product or that it will eventually just fail. But what they don't want is to pay $150 for something that just covers stains or is never going to be used, that's being sold to them by an associate with no passion or belief in what they are presenting. What they are really in need of is peace of mind, or a worry-free experience at pennies on the dollar. They need someone with confidence to lead them who also has a belief that this product will truly make their lives easier.

Most of my counterparts were calling the program a warranty and selling it at the counter at the last minute. There was no attention being paid to the program's inherent value. It was looked upon as an obligatory hassle. I remember many of my counterparts saying, "I just don't sell it because I forget all the time."

Not me. I chose to retool the pitch to what I now call "building the value proposition."

Instead of asking for an additional $150, I broke down the cost of the five-year protection program and would present it as $2.50 per month or eight cents per day. I would highlight all the issues that occur in everyday life and use their own examples, like children or a particular job or a type of lifestyle, to highlight the benefits of this effortless protection plan *in their lives* protecting against the inevitable. But most importantly, I would present this program early and often throughout the sale and with lots of passion and enthusiasm. I cannot stress enough how important it is to have some energy behind the pitch— something to show the customer you believe in this. If so, when you are combining it all together, you greatly increase your chance of finalizing the deal.

Within sixty days at the furniture store I had bypassed my base pay—easily making more money than my guarantee, but also making more money on a regular basis than I had made my entire life.

ALL THAT WORK PAID OFF

I used all the skills I built and continued working on them daily. One weekend it paid off big. The owner announced a big sales contest for furniture sales and protection plans. The contest was from Friday through Monday, which was Labor Day if I remember correctly. The top protection plan writer would receive a $500 bonus, plus be paid their regular 20 percent commission. And whoever wrote the most furniture sales would also win Rose Room box seats to the Portland Trail Blazers game that Monday night, all expenses paid. This was a huge deal, as our company sponsored the Blazers basketball team. Everyone wanted to win that prize.

I was never the top writer in that organization. Usually I was number two or three or sometimes even the fourth highest writer out of twelve. I was, however, regularly number one or two in protection plan sales and decided to use that to my advantage. The contest began and I remember the top writer telling me that he would never let me win the contest and that he was going to pull out all the stops to ensure his victory. This guy delivered furniture in his own truck for free to make deals. He stood in dresser drawers to demonstrate quality. He did *whatever* it took to make a sale. As such, I had never beaten the top writer on the sales floor.

There was lots of boasting and side-eye going around all weekend, as the twelve of us constantly monitored one another's sales.

By day two, the usual top writer and I were back and forth in the top spot with a steady lead over the rest of the sales associates. By Sunday night, with only one day to go, he and I were neck and neck on furniture sales, but I was significantly in the lead on protection plan sales. The competition was crazy and so much fun.

At three p.m. on Monday, the owner cut off the contest to announce the winner. That person would get their bonus cash and be off to the game with anyone they wanted to take.

I won *both* the top sales for the four days and the protection plan contest—selling just under $39,000 in furniture and $2,450 in protection plans. My payout for the four days was:

Furniture ($39,000 at 6 percent commission): $2,340

Protection ($2,450 at 20 percent commission): $490

Bonus: $500

Rose Room tickets at the Rose Garden: priceless!

$3,330 for four days of work to me was like winning the lottery. Understand that just four months before, I was working three jobs making maybe $1,300 to $1,500 per month.

By the way, I only beat the top writer by $900 dollars in furniture sales. It was the protection plans that pushed me over the top and made all the difference in the close contest.

To win, I figured out that I had to maximize the clients I had. I asked probing questions to qualify clients quickly. The owner promoted heavy that week for the event and opened the floor to a free-for-all. Many sales floors have what's called an "up system," which is a way for each sales associate to work with one customer at a time in a specific order. But during this sale the gloves were off and the floor was open, so no up system. This created a tough sales environment and you really had to be on your game to write business. When I found someone, I had to be very concise on the questions and work to build the value to close the deal quickly. Once I had a client that wanted to buy, I really worked on promoting protection plans early. It was a *long* weekend and I worked opening bell to closing each day, which gave me and the top writer—who always did that on holiday weekends—an advantage. In my first four months, I strategically took on the best of the skills I witnessed from other sales associates and avoided the bad. As result of observing, learning, and executing, I was well on my way to a decent career in selling.

It's interesting how, at least in some sales jobs, one can see that you will get out what you put in. I watched many people come and go in my sales career—many people who would show up to work smelling like alcohol or show up late all the time yet still somehow manage to eke out a living. Many people brought bad attitudes and lots of complaining and they still all made a living. But the ones that were truly at the top seemed to outwork everyone by simply hustling and moving faster. They had energy and attitude about them—a sense of urgency. It's truly amazing to watch it in action.

Valuable lessons were learned that long contest weekend and cost me nothing. I was really no one before that weekend, and now I was on the radar.

ON THE MOVE AGAIN

Only a few short months after the contest I won, the store announced it was going out of business. Thankfully I was offered a position on another sales team by my old friend Travis, whom I met when I was fifteen. The job was to travel with them all over the country and sell hot tubs at trade shows and fairs. I really had my doubts. First, was I *qualified* to do this? And can you really make a living on the road selling hot tubs? Well, I was soon to find out, as I really did not have a choice. My roommate at the time had met his soul mate and moved out, leaving me hanging with his share of our rent.

I moved in with one of the closing store's office people and his family, sleeping on yet another couch. I had to think hard about where I would go next. I was thankful to have a place to sleep at the last minute—and being relatively new to Portland, did not have many options—but I remember thinking, as I slept on the couch with their stuff piled up everywhere around me and their baby crying every night for hours, *Here we go again. Why can't I get a break and just have some security in my life? No more couches and feeling like a burden on others. This sucks.*

I really had to channel my past to drive me in the right direction, but it was hard to stay positive and optimistic. What got me through was remembering that I had been in far worse positions.

A few days later I met with Travis at the airport and he showed me a check for $9,800 that he had just earned from a six-day show. I could not believe it. He said he would be off for about a week and then back at it in another state for a four-day show where he would likely gross another $3,000 or so. Any uncertainty I had about the hot tub sales job disappeared. I officially took the offered position.

With Travis's blessing, I moved back to southern Oregon and in with him to start a career selling hot tubs on the road. He was right; we made a ton of money. My best show was during a ten-day period wherein at the age of twenty-two I made just under $9,500. It felt like crazy cash for a twenty-two-year-old with no college education or even high school diploma. I really began to believe I had found my calling. Travis's father, who was our boss, said that I was a natural and could sell with them forever. Travis and I had a good system of team selling and sometimes bringing in his dad to close deals. His father was larger than life at more than six feet, four inches tall, 275 pounds of muscle—a monster in stature, but truly a gentle giant and a good salesman. I learned from them what high pressure sales was all about. I mean, think about it. We were flown in to nowhere Michigan to work the state fair. There was competition all around. We competed in a booth with thirty to forty hot tubs, against the local stores' less-skilled sales representatives who worked for the owner who flew us in for the show to help handle the much higher volume traffic. The first time I did this, I thought they were nuts. But I'll be dammed, at my first big show our team of three sold fifty-three hot tubs in ten days. Any fear I had going into this profession was dwarfed by the confidence I built during and after that experience. It was a wild time. We were sweating in our slacks and dress shirts. There were tornado warnings. It was lonely being on the road. And this was a rough area of Michigan to top it all off. But we succeeded.

BONUS POINT: I want to take a minute to highlight the importance of facing your fears. Fear is really just the unknown. I read once that we were born to survive, not succeed. That made a lot of sense to me because if we let fear drive our decisions all the time there would not be much progress in our lives. To excel and advance, you must not just face the fear but understand it's natural. Go after what you fear and embrace it. What do you have to lose? If everything was provided to you or if you had enough to survive, you wouldn't work much harder. But if you don't have enough, you may push harder or sometime even face fear to get what you need.

Most people would rather not face fear. They do not want to push through adversity because it's hard, scary, and unknown. I say just do it to see what happens and you may find a great reward on the other side.

After a while I moved on from the hot tub sales gig because the dynamic began to change in the team. High-volume home shows were the moneymakers but, unlike my counterpart, I was being sent to mall stores to work.

I followed up with the owner of the last furniture store I worked at because I heard he was opening a new store. He was happy to hear from me and offered a position as a sales associate (with the promise of it evolving into the store manager once I learned the system). I accepted.

While working at this store I had one of the best sales experiences I ever had, while facing one of the worst and most challenging months in selling. I was on my way to a terrible pay period. I had not sold well during that time and the pay period ended on a Sunday. It was already Wednesday and I was running out of time. I remember it like it was yesterday. After complaining a little to the owner about the store traffic and lack of advertising, he told me to stay positive and focused because I still had lots of customers to work with before Sunday and must treat all of them like they are my last.

DON'T JUDGE—IT'S NOT RIGHT (AND CAN LITERALLY COST YOU MONEY)

It was about eleven a.m., and I was the second sales associate up and the next customer was mine. My up (customer) walked in and it was a middle-aged woman dressed in business casual clothes. I introduced myself and asked what product I could help her find. She said she was just looking for a full-size mattress. I looked back at the owner as if to say, *I told you so*, with a smirk on my face.

Her name was Zina. I spent about ten minutes talking with her and found her to be a very pleasant person, so I relaxed and started to work through the selling process, even though I really thought it was going to be a waste of time. As she lay on one mattress and I on another, we chatted about life in general and then she began to share a lot of detail: She was recently divorced, she paid cash for her new Mercedes, she just bought a five-thousand-square foot house in a wealthy area down the freeway from the store, and *she needed to furnish the entire house.* By the time Zina left the store at about three p.m. she had bought about $40,000 worth of merchandise.

I delivered it personally with the drivers that weekend. While I was there, I worked with her on artwork, rugs, and other accessories to add to the sale. She referred in at least three friends who spent an additional $10,000, and they were wonderful people to deal with. The fact that a mattress customer ended up being a $50,000 customer taught me never to pre-judge any customer in the future. Plus, she helped me rock a huge paycheck when I really needed it. Zina told me later that she only picked our store because the name Smart and Quick Furniture made her feel like she could get a quick, cheap mattress for one of her kids who was sleeping on the floor of their new empty home. She would have otherwise never shopped in our type of store.

I'll never forget I was able to turn around a potential sale of a full-size promotional mattress at $299 ($18 commission) into $50,000 in sales ($3,000 commission)— all from good training and sticking to my presentation and professional approach. It's easy in sales to get down and pre-judge, but you cannot do that, as you never know who you're dealing with.

I HAD A FIRE INSIDE AND IT WAS TELLING ME TO GO FOR IT

As promised, I was soon the general manager and running the store, but something was missing. I really wanted a challenge beyond what I was doing and was not sure of the future of the business based on the history of the operator. I felt I had reached the max potential at that store in my current position and it was time to move on. I heard that a local furniture representative might be hiring an associate to work with him. This rep, Steve, worked as an independent contractor for a mid-size furniture company selling wholesale goods to the local furniture stores. I'd watched for years how the reps interacted with the owners of stores, so I thought there might be a big opportunity to jump up to the next level and work on the wholesale side of things. Most of these reps were well-dressed and drove nice cars. I, too, really wanted more in life and was inspired by what they were doing. I could not have explained it at the time, but there was something in me that drove me to keep pushing forward—not just because I wanted more money, but a drive to challenge myself to grab what was attainable. I felt capable of more.

To interview for the position, I had to resign as the store manager and go back to a sales position, taking a pay cut as to not jeopardize the relationship between the owner and sales rep at the time. I did that and thought, *Well, it's all or nothing at this point.*

The day I had my interview, I wore a suit I bought in a package deal with the tie and shirt for $79. It was my first suit. I prepared like crazy for the interview—what to say and what to bring. I did mock interviews with a friend who asked lots of questions. I instinctively felt that this was a big opportunity and thus trained as if for a Super Bowl. At the interview I must have looked so overzealous and a little desperate. I was all in.

Afterward, Steve told me two things: 1) the job paid $2,800 per month, and 2) I could not continue living with another company's associate who was Steve's direct competition and a conflict of interest in his eyes. So . . . take about a 30 to 40 percent pay cut from my current job *and* find another place to live? Okay, I would find a way to make it work. I just wanted the opportunity, as I had a feeling it would pay off in the long run. I asked him if there was anything I could do or provide him to assist in his decision. He said, "No, you've prepared so much that I didn't take a single note." His pad was blank next to a folder I had provided with references, a letter of intent, and my short résumé. He said he would decide in the next few weeks after a few more interviews.

I called Steve almost every day for weeks just to check in—always positive and upbeat, letting him know how much the potential opportunity meant to me. I told him I would not let him down if he just gave me the chance to prove myself.

Finally, I got the call I had been waiting for when Steve offered me the job.

"You were the most prepared and persistent person I have ever interviewed," he said. "And the reason I'm giving you the job is so you will stop calling me about it." He told me that I drove him crazy. We had a great laugh over that and I assured him he would not regret his decision.

Being an associate was a whole new ball game, and my boss was both very good and very serious. I remember him telling me on my first day at a furniture show in San Francisco, "You see that guy? He's a VP and you are never to look at or say anything to him."

What did I get myself into?

As part of taking the job as a new associate working for Steve, I moved into the attic of one of the sales associates I had worked with, who was close to retirement. Yes, I moved into *an attic* for $400 per month, but I did not care because I was going to make it big and get out of that attic in short order.

Just before the job, I had purchased an Audi sports car, so I kind of looked like I knew what I was doing, at least from the outside. I appeared to have money and should not be living in an attic. I can remember the person I was renting from just beside herself at how I explained to my dates how living in the attic had its advantages and that it was my *choice* to live there. Little did everyone know, it could not be further from the truth. Let's recap.

I was living in an attic. I had at least $700 in monthly auto and insurance expenses. I just took a pay cut of 30 to 40 percent to take a new job working for an individual I barely knew. And I had poor credit.

Sounds like a path to success to me.

PRINCIPLED LEADERSHIP

Steve taught me how to be a professional. He was very good at what he does and had a strong system for providing the best possible outcome at every sales call. He was driven by his principles, including that the client was the most important priority in his day. He demonstrated that every time we worked together, showing me how important it was to check the warehouse and solve any issues the clients may have had before we met with the buyers. He would check with the sales associates and make sure they knew how important they were to us and tell them how much we appreciated them. We would make diligent notes on what was missing from the floors and make notes on the suggested item we wanted to present. He was great at problem-solving, and the clients really respected him. He even worked private events and held sales trainings constantly.

I attribute some of my success today to Steve's mentoring and I'm fortunate to have been given the opportunity to work with him. It's funny, before I started working for him all I knew of reps was that they took my bosses out to lunch and sold them a few things. But I would soon learn that Steve was not a rep; he was a marketing specialist and held in high regard by his clients. I wanted to be like that. After working with him for two years, there was a clear difference between the two types of salesmen.

TO INCORPORATE OR NOT TO INCORPORATE

For the first few years working for Steve, I was not making much money, so I chose to just keep my receipts in a shoebox and pay my taxes at the end of the year—basically like a sole proprietor. Later in my career, I did start several LLCs (Limited Liability Company) and an S

Corp. There are advantages to all these, and you will need to seek the proper advice from a certified public accountant if you want to set it up correctly.

I was asked once by some married friends if I had some advice on how they could make more money. First, I asked why they needed to make more money. They told me one of them was making good money with his new job but they had now been moved up to the next tax bracket and lots of taxes were being taken out, causing financial strain. I sat them down and asked, "How much do you spend and where do you spend it?" Once we broke down the spending habits and worked on how we could eliminate some waste, we then started brainstorming what she could do to bring in additional income. She was a stay-at-home mom and the thought was if she could add a revenue stream while maximizing write-offs as an independent business owner, coupled with getting a handle on spending, they would be on their way. Soon after that conversation she started an LLC for her Mary Kay business, and it not only brought in extra income, but also maximized the write-offs more than offsetting the tax loss from his new position. Plus, she's having a blast doing it.

There are often straightforward ways to solve your financial issues, but I recommend you do a few things first:

1) Educate yourself on the topic using books, podcasts, and websites. Commit to putting in the work.
2) Set financial goals and get on the same page with your significant other.
3) Identify where every penny of your money is spent.
4) Find ways to utilize the tax write-offs.
5) Add another source of income. You won't believe how many there are.
6) Celebrate the small wins and regularly measure your achievements.

Without a plan, you can't measure. Without measuring, you can't achieve. And if you're not achieving, what's the point?

PUT IN EFFORT LIKE YOUR FINANCIAL LIFE DEPENDS ON IT

Armed with a strong work ethic and and the sheer determination to be the best associate I could possibly be, I had success working for several business owners. I read every book that Steve and the company we represented suggested. I studied the other senior reps at the furniture markets. I got coffee for anyone that needed it and some who did not (they thought that was weird). I did everything I could to make life easier for those around us when traveling to furniture markets, and worked extra hard for the clients we called on. I worked many private sales on my own time, unloaded trucks, trained sales associates, and went above and beyond in any way I could. The goal was to make them feel like they wanted me around all the time. If I could do this, then I would likely get orders when other reps were pushed away.

While working for Steve, I read two books that laid the foundation for my selling career. The first was *Hope Is Not a Strategy: The 6 Keys to Winning the Complex Sale* by Rick Page. He really dives in to linking solutions to pain or gain. This is really good and can help solve problems for your clients, and as a result you may earn their business. The second was *SPIN Selling* by Neil Rackham. This book taught me the single most important thing I use to this day. Rackham calls it the "Value Equation." This involves building enough value to exceed the price, putting you in the best position to earn the sale.

BONUS POINT: When a leader in your organization suggests you read a book, I recommend you do it. Many of these books taught me critical skills, and eventually led me toward searching for more knowledge. (Thanks, Kerry, for all those suggestions.)

I was so excited and thankful to be part of this new world. My work was my life and all I wanted was to drive business for my boss and the company. Steve approached me one day and asked if I would like to take advantage of an opportunity to cover a larger area of his territory. He offered me 50 percent more pay and a bit more freedom. The only caveat was that I had to move out of state to Washington in two weeks. His other associate was moving on to pursue his lifelong passion of becoming a firefighter. I did not hesitate to say yes. Here we go again—on the move, but for a fantastic opportunity. I packed all my stuff and said good-bye to the attic.

I worked this new area for a little more than a year when the absolute worst-case scenario occurred. Steve was notified by corporate that his territory was being cut and he must take only one of the two states he covered. For some reason the company would not give me an opportunity to take one of them but instead hired someone outside our company. Steve tried to tell them that he would mentor me to take over Washington, but they had made their decision. I can only guess that the decision was based on my relative lack of experience and young age or maybe the fact that Steve's VP was new to the company and may have been influenced by other factors. But either way, one of Steve's associates was going to lose his job after an upcoming show.

Steve, the other associate, and I got a bottle of whisky and drank as we shared memories of our time working together. I'm not going to lie, I teared up. I was so passionate about working for this company, I would have done anything for them. I just wished they could see that. I was absolutely devastated. It seemed like every time in my life I was getting things together, I would be kicked in the stomach and knocked down. This was one of the hardest. I just could not believe it; it was so unfair.

Today, I do not believe in the term "unfair," but back then I remember feeling that way. I don't believe anything is fair or unfair. We are not entitled to anything and sometimes things just happen, and it is what it is. You really must decide if you are going to be a victim or turn your circumstances into an opportunity. Fair and unfair is a choice—at least the action coming out of the circumstance is anyway.

I was told by Steve that he could bring me back to Oregon with a pay cut, but then he would have to cut the current Oregon associate loose. I did not want to put him in that position and thought this may be a good opportunity to try opening my own furniture store. So, I did.

NOT QUITE AS GLAMOROUS AS I THOUGHT

I opened my store in an empty location of a building I had worked in before. I had a little capital but really opened taking a huge risk. The store had a one-year lease because the shopping center was up for possible redevelopment. I will fast-forward through this part. I worked seven days a week, taking only half days off a few times in the one-year period. I even worked on Thanksgiving and Christmas Day, setting the floor while the store itself was closed. It was a year of tons of challenging work and stress. When the lease was up for renewal, I realized sitting in one place, working hours I could not even count, and running this store on my own, was *not* a good fit for me. We liquidated, paid off the vendors, and I was back on the market looking for work.

BONUS POINT: Running a retail business is *very* hard work. If you are thinking about it, you'd better do your research, work for free in a similar environment to what you want to open, build a good business plan, and make sure your starting capital is large enough to cover any unforeseen issues. If you don't at least do this, then forget it. Don't even start.

FAMILIAR FRIENDS AND NEW OPPORTUNITIES

I was having dinner and interviewing with a retail store owner in Washington when I received a phone call from my friend Nick, who was a senior marketing specialist for a different division of the same manufacturer I used to work for. He and my old boss Steve were now contractors working for this company. We had worked closely together when I was in Washington in past years. Now he asked me if I wanted to partner with him in his business. He needed help because he had just lost his associate. He said he really appreciated my work ethic and attitude when we worked together and thought we might be a good fit. Nick also lacked the retail experience I had and thought that would add immense value to his business.

It felt good to hear someone say that I would add value to their company after being pushed aside a year earlier by another one that I worked so hard for, and then basically failing at running my own store. I was not in a good place mentally at the time he offered me this opportunity, but his encouragement reinvigorated me.

BONUS POINT: Never burn a bridge and always give it your all in life. You never know when an opportunity may just fall out of the sky as a result of an interaction you may have not thought twice about.

Nick's call reinforced my belief that you cannot get down when things don't go your way. I could not have seen it at the time, but the challenges in my life were necessary in developing who I would become and would drive me to enormous success later in life. I truly believe that you must fail, fall, crash, and struggle to have and appreciate success or effectiveness in whatever you do. I'm not saying that a few people in life who were either handed a business, a bunch of money, or maybe have never failed, do not work hard or appreciate what they have. But those of us who had nothing and built something from nothing have a different perspective—a different respect and appreciation for it. I know this because I have personally dealt with people from both sides of this equation many times in my life.

For instance, I remember a manager in his sixties telling me how his mom would bring ice cream to his room, and if the fruit in it was not right, he would send her back to the kitchen to fix it. He told me this after I shared my upbringing with him. He said it in the context of having it really easy as a kid and that he basically got whatever he wanted while growing up. I didn't want to judge, but I remember thinking how ridiculous that sounded. I was living off food stamps and sugar bread while getting jumped by gangs as a kid, and this guy sends his ice cream back to Mommy because it had the wrong fruit in it? The moral of the story is that we experience different circumstances as children, but here we both were having a conversation about our youth and our different perspectives and that was okay. We were two complete opposites getting along just fine.

TIME TO STEP UP MY GAME

As business partners, Nick and I constantly sought to educate and improve ourselves. One of the first books we read as partners to keep our business on track was *The Toyota Way* by Jeffrey K. Liker. In the book, Liker talks a lot about efficiency, eliminating waste, and continually solving problems. The book really set the tone on what type of company we wanted to be. I've now read it several times, and it's an essential book about an amazing company.

For about a year or two, I ramped up my self-education, focusing on self-improvement and business development. Some books were provided by companies we contracted with as suggested reads, but many were found through research. I began to develop a thirst for knowledge—ultimately reading more than one hundred books in the next seven years. In addition to books, I studied computer programs like Microsoft Office and Adobe Illustrator to better help me understand the numbers and presentation options, specifically the Excel program. I would learn that numbers don't lie and can give you a great understanding of where to go in your business.

We also attended some Harry Freidman sales training courses and other seminars. It was very beneficial to partner with someone who had different strengths than I did. Nick and I learned a lot from each other and it showed. We won a sales contest for the company we represented. We built business plans that were up to twenty pages long, and regularly executed our goals while achieving double-digit growth. We worked constantly—sometimes seven days per week. We would construct showroom displays, going above and beyond the client's expectation—even paying for the props out of our own pocket. We literally had the keys to a few of our clients' stores because they trusted us so much.

Together, we held lots of sales trainings and built manuals that we shared with the company. We even worked retail floors on weekends for free when we were not busy with another work-related task. Overall, we did whatever it took to drive our clients' business and it paid off big.

We were having a spectacular year in business. I was renting the top floor of Nick's house and then I was shocked to hear from one of my counterparts that the senior marketing specialist (or rep) position Steve tried to help me get was about to reopen. The person who filled "my" Washington position was moving on. I still really wanted that job, and now, just two years later, it's going to be available. I worked for the same company in a different capacity as a partnership in a different division, but I thought to myself, *Here's my shot and I'm not letting it slip through my hands this time.* I had been working hard building presentation for the division and trying to make a difference. I developed a good reputation as a team player and had built several relationships at the time across the entire company in hopes that maybe *someday* I could earn a position with the company as a senior marketing specialist.

My time had come.

I was interviewed by the same person who would not give me an interview the first time the position had opened. Back then I thought for sure I would be giving at least an interview but no go. Now, two things were certain: The guy they hired was moving on, and I was considered a worthy candidate. It would have been easy to have animosity and hard feelings toward the company and the people that were part of that decision a few years back, but that made no sense. No hard feelings, as this was about to be the interview of my life, no doubt.

BONUS POINT: No one is entitled to anything and there are many reasons decisions are made. Many factors steer corporate decisions and you may not always be informed. As I have said before, it's better to use the energy when you are knocked down to fight, improve, and get better, because something will eventually happen for you. The universe has a way of rewarding those who work hard and keep pushing forward with no excuses. Just keep going. You cannot control those around you, but you can control your actions, and sometimes the results of those actions.

I prepared for the interview, and when we finished, I humbly said, "I have been with this company for several years now, even supporting it with a store when I left by selling its products and eventually coming back in another division. I'm a fighter and I bleed this company's colors. I will work every day as though it's my last if I'm just given an opportunity. Please let me prove it to you."

The interviewer called me the next day, and not only offered me the prized position, but said, "I have no doubt that you will work hard for us. I'm giving you this job because I should have given it to you the first time. And you've earned it."

There are no sweeter words to hear (and recognize as true) than *you've earned it.*

During the last year I was business partners with Nick, I was making pretty good money. I remember being so proud of that. I flew down to California to visit my grandmother, who was suffering from the initial stages of Alzheimer's disease. I really wanted to share my excitement with her. I gave her a $100 bill and said, "Grandma, I've made it. I'm making six figures now." I remember her asking, "What is six figures?" but she was excited about the $100. Obviously, money is not everything, but my grandmother knew of my struggles as a kid and I just wanted her to know I was doing okay. I was so thankful for all her earlier sacrifices for me and only wish she could have seen more of what I had accomplished.

CHAPTER NINE

DON'T LET MONEY GO
TO YOUR HEAD

T HE FEW YEARS I lived and worked with Nick, I developed a bit of arrogance as I let the money and success I was having go to my head. I bought a Rolex watch, drove a nice red Audi with custom wheels, and spent lots of money while traveling on superficial things like VIP rooms at clubs and fancy dinners. For a brief time, I totally forgot my past and how hard it was to get where I landed.

My far more grounded girlfriend, Christina, and I had broken up a few times and I was losing my way a bit. I remember she once found a $2,900 receipt on my dresser for one night's fun of VIP rooms. Even split among friends, the extravagance did not look good. Man, she was angry when she found that. I watched several people around me buy big expensive homes and luxury cars. They took off on lavish vacations and really just spent a lot on nothing important. Under this influence, it was difficult to stay focused on my finances. What an idiot I was—buying Rolex watches and spending *thousands* in dance clubs. Thankfully, it did not last long, as the finance books I began to read were a major wake-up call.

BONUS POINT: When you see people showing off all their fancy stuff and living in places that seem unreal, it's important to understand that only a small percentage of them can actually afford that stuff. Don't use that stuff or those people as a beacon to lead you on a path to success. You will quickly find that it's a slippery slope that may take you decades to recover from.

Soon after I sold the Rolex online and only lost about $300 from the original purchase price, and stopped spending like crazy. Nick hooked me up with an accountant, who set me up with a retirement plan and QuickBooks accounting software. The accountant helped me to see what I was spending, and the retirement account saved me money on taxes while making me money on the investment.

BONUS POINT: If you're dealing with overspending issues:

1. Work to understand the spending habit.
2. Identify what drives the spending issue.
3. Determine how all the money is being spent.
4. Detail how it affects you and your family, and work to illustrate the eventual consequences if the spending continues.
5. Put together a plan to help the person with the spending habit get it under control.
6. Hold people accountable by measuring the results and—good or bad—address them.

Solutions can range from a spending tracker on a spreadsheet or app to closing all accounts to introducing new hobbies or swapping downtime with productive time, but communication and having *both* sides on board and working toward the solution is key.

GET YOUR FINANCIAL HOUSE IN ORDER

At twenty-seven years old, I still did not have one dollar saved and yet I was making more money than at any time in my life. I wish I would have talked with an accountant sooner or read a book specifically about money. In the first post-accountant and retirement plan year, I invested

$12,000 into a retirement account and saved $9,000 in cash. By year two I had invested $24,000 and saved $15,000 in cash.

After all I went through growing up, and the general lack of money in my life, you would think that maybe I would have appreciated the financial success I was having and saved for a rainy day before this point. But we all see things through a different prism and can be influenced by what's around us. I would have been further along financially if I had spent some earlier time investing in learning about the value of money. I was fortunate to have crossed paths with a few mentors who built up my confidence, character, and work ethic, but I underestimated the value of being financially smart.

After saving money, the next step was to buy my own home, and at the beginning of year three I did. I was super excited to be buying my first home because I felt it would give me a sense of security to finally have a home to call my own. It really meant a lot to me. I would never sleep on a couch again.

To this day I have a tough time staying at other people's houses. I'm very uncomfortable with it and feel like I'm putting someone out. Even though I will likely never have to stay with someone again, the impact of all that couch surfing growing up has had a long-lasting effect.

One of the books I bought to learn more about money is called *The Truth About Money* by Ric Edelman. It's a lengthy book but is a must-read to better understand the power of what your money can do for you. He talks about planning, reserve funds, stocks, mortgages, managing risk, and insurance to name a few. If you want to make the most of your money and better understand how to make it work for you, *The Truth About Money* is a good start.

The same week I bought my new home I bought a new car: a 2007 Lexus RX350. These are very reliable and great for traveling sales reps. I bought the car new after a ton of research and knew I would drive it till the wheels fell off. I chose the vehicle based on reliability and resale, not on looks. Admittedly I wanted a cooler-looking SUV, but knew the cost of overall ownership would not make as much sense. I spent a lot of time researching purchases and it made a significant difference. For instance, I bought my home in a modest neighborhood even though I was mortgage-approved for a house that cost well more than what I paid for mine. I intentionally wanted to stay in a comfort zone in case something happened with my job.

I paid $273,000 for my home and $43,000 for my car. I know what you are thinking. He bought all that *after* getting an accountant and learning from his mistakes? Yes, while this may seem like a stupid move, it worked out well, and there were a few lessons learned with these purchases.

My brand-new home was purchased in the summer of 2006 at the peak of the real-estate bubble, so by 2011 my home value had dropped to $215,000. Ouch. But I did not foreclose and walk away. I stayed with it and refinanced it a few times. After a few years, and paying a little more down, I was able to refinance at a rate of 2.75 percent, now owing $158,000 with a current value of $338,000. I moved out of the home to buy another. I refinanced my original home so I could rent it. The home now rents for $1,895 with a mortgage of $1,200—creating passive cash flow of about $600 per month after expenses. All this while my renter pays the house payment and an equity position of about $180,000 that increases each year.

Not bad for a house that was worth 25 percent less than what I paid for it at one point.

The Lexus that I paid $43,000 for in the summer of 2006 I still own today, and it has approximately 435,000 miles on it. I paid it off in mid 2012. So, the cost of ownership was about $5,500 per year because of how long I owned it and minimal maintenance costs which included tax, payment, insurance, and upkeep. I'm in the process of selling the car under its value at $2,000, so let's deduct that. Now the overall cost of ownership is down to $5,344 annually. You must account for the fuel cost because that's not a write-off when you deduct mileage, so that was $3,000 per year or $250 per month. This brings the cost of ownership per year back up to $8,344. Then while owning it I was able to write off an average of $0.54 per mile, so let's say 290,000 business miles driven at $0.54 per mile equals a write-off totaling $157,140 over a twelve-year period or $13,095 per year. This means I did not have to pay the 28 percent tax on this amount of money each year and it was treated as a deduction on my taxes.

What all this means is when I started my new career as a senior marketing specialist and started my new LLC in 2006, I was able to write off and deduct my vehicle as a business expense.

All these calculations above show I drove a nice car that was very reliable for twelve years and in the end—after fuel, maintenance, car payments, taxes, and insurance—I made $8,751 per year (or $729.25 per month) to drive a Lexus. Yes, that's right I was paid through tax deductions to drive my car and was able to save six years of payments after it was paid off on top of the tax write-off advantage.

Under non-business circumstances, or in the case where a person buys a new car every three years, an average vehicle would have cost $8,698 (or $725 per month) as a cost of ownership. The Lexus purchase showed a break-even compared to other vehicles on cost of ownership without the business write-offs, but you could be driving a Lexus, and with the low maintenance after year six start saving those payments. This break-even is only because I have a three-times higher fuel cost with my travel schedule. An average driver would save using my example by owning this car for twelve years. Now I could have bought a used Lexus—which I did on my next purchase and feel will be an even better return—but my new purchase in 2006 worked out fine.

My Lexus payment was $719 per month, so after six years I put $719 in a savings account as if I still had a car payment. And that amount saved was approximately $51,000. In the book *The Millionaire Next Door* by Thomas J. Stanley, Ph.D. and William D. Danko, Ph.D., there is a great chapter called "You Aren't What You Drive" and this goes in-depth about millionaires and their vehicle purchasing habits. It's a terrific book.

IMPORTANCE OF TRACKING YOUR EXPENSES AND NET WORTH

I converted my Chris Roberts and Associates, LLC (which I started about 2006) into Fusion Sales and Marketing, Inc., which more fully encompassed what my company was doing at the time. I started reading more books about money and investing, and built a spreadsheet to track all my expenses. It's important to track where all your money goes so you can manage it, and then create your own financial opportunities. A few things I learned were:

1) Track all your expenses, so you can see how wasteful you are. It's alarming, believe me.

2) Cut cost anywhere possible. It's easy to do when you measure.

3) No amount of money is too small to start automatically transferring to your savings and investing accounts. Make it a routine and you won't even miss it.

4) Pay yourself first: emergency fund, vacation fund, savings, and investments. This will allow you to relax when it's time to retire.

5) Avoid credit cards and payment plans of any kind if possible, as you will pay twice as much for things you will soon not care about.

6) Don't "keep up with the Joneses"—they don't care about you. Instead, live below your means. You will be glad you did at some point in your life.

7) Create multiple streams of income—and when you make more money save it, because a storm is coming.

Today I'm implementing some systems and processes to measure and track my finances. I monitor my personal and business checking accounts almost daily and run my credit report every six months. I review my written goals and hold myself accountable to how the progress is going. Eventually I started using Mint.com for basic tracking, but I had a spreadsheet when I first started.

When you sign up with a finance tracker like Mint, it's much easier to manage getting out of debt or building your reserves if you have little debt to start. It does not matter if you work for $7 per hour or make $100,000 per year—if you are not tracking, it will be very difficult to build wealth or to eventually become financially free. I know an individual who makes $4,500 per month who vacations in beautiful places all over the world every year, has a savings of more than $40,000 built up, all while living a stress-free life. On the other hand, I know someone making $200,000 per year who lives paycheck to paycheck with zero savings, lots of expenses, and is living a stressful life. When you prioritize and measure your life, you write your own ticket.

It's also important if you want to build wealth to track your net worth. Your net worth is the value of what you have, like property, cash, retirement, and other assets in total after deducting what you owe in mortgages, credit card bills, and debts in general. I'm a big fan of tracking net worth because you can watch your investments grow while trimming down expenses. You will gain momentum and encouragement as your net worth grows, and then you can take it to the next level. From here you can work on finding tax write-off opportunities or work to create more streams of income. Just continue to make your money work as it grows. You may even reinvest in other business opportunities.

Sites like Mint will show you where you're spending your money with category trackers and how your net worth is growing, keeping you accountable to both your spending and savings habits.

BONUS POINT: Please think about how difficult it will be when you get older if you have nothing saved—no reserves, no assets to draw cash from, or maybe you're one of the millions of people like me that will not have a pension to fall back on. Perhaps Social Security does not exist down the road or it's for the select few that really need it, leaving you out. I want you to visualize what it will be like when medical bills start coming in or a hardship hits you from the ages of sixty to eighty and you have no way of dealing with it. You must think about a time in your life when you will not have the same energy to work like you do in your twenties, thirties, or forties. You must put yourself in the frame of mind of a time when life will not be as carefree and fruitful as it is today. Scare yourself straight and get on track because then you will be ready for the inevitable. If you plan and commit, a little sacrifice today will give you an unbelievable lifeline when you need it.

One example of how I lowered my financial stress is when Christina and I got married. (More about Christina later.) We agreed we would have a long engagement to save enough money to have her dream wedding. We saved for two and a half years and when we were close to our budget we got married on the beach of a private estate in Hawaii and we still had $1,700 left in the account. It was the happiest day in our lives, because we loved each other *and* because we had no debt coming out of it.

Something I do in addition to writing down goals and tracking is to surround myself with a positive environment. I had canvas art made of all the mountains I've climbed put on my wall outside my office. I have a portrait of who, in my mind, was the most influential president of all time on my wall between the mountains. And I have positive and encouraging sayings posted all over the office. All these things remind me daily of what we are capable of, and it's an important exercise that's kept me in the correct mind-set.

CHAPTER TEN

GIVING BACK AND GOING FORWARD

I CONTINUED WORKING HARD, filling in most of my free time going to self-improvement seminars, listening to podcasts, and watching webinars. I even went back to school and received my GED, then took a few classes at the local college to improve my writing skills. I spent countless hours late at night working on presentations for my team, but I also did whatever I could to help the larger company. True to my promise to the interviewer, I'm so passionate about my work and the company I represent. I worked many of the next years showing up days early to furniture shows to build showroom presentations and assisted wherever I could. Sometimes I worked on charity events, generating thousands of dollars that I would donate on behalf of the team. Because of that personal growth and development, I was honored by winning the Rookie of the Year award in 2007 and the Marketing Specialist of the Year award in 2010. This second award was very meaningful to me because it was voted on by more than eighty-five of my peers, and I really appreciated that they chose me.

HOW I BECAME A RESERVE POLICE OFFICER

As I read more and gained more life experience, I really wanted to give back. I was growing as an individual, and for the better. My future wife, Christina, and I were then engaged, and I could not be happier. I went on a ride-along with a police officer because I wanted to learn more about the community I was living in and when that ride-along was over I was hooked. It was amazing to see how the officers interacted with the public, but especially with the children. I did not have the best experience growing up around police, but that perception was shattered in just one night as I rode along with that lead officer. I began to see police in a whole new light.

After the shift, the lieutenant asked me if I would be interested in becoming a reserve police officer. I shared a few details about my life with him and he felt that my experiences while growing up and later running a business could help the community. I went home and did a ton of research and was soon convinced becoming a reserve officer was something I had to do. I trained like crazy, physically and mentally, beating out dozens of other candidates in the physical agility, written testing, and interview processes. After I was selected, I went through a four-month police academy, attending class on nights and weekends before graduating as a commissioned police officer. Most reserves use this program to give them an advantage when applying for a full-time position, but I went through the grueling qualification process just to volunteer. I did it just to give back, learn about my community, and be on the team.

While in the academy, I really developed my courage and leadership. I was a squad leader and—just like at work—volunteered first for everything I could: to get tasered, to fight for life (an intense, simulated fight to test you physically), to clear a dark building, etc. At the reserve academy graduation ceremony, I was honored with the Outstanding Service Award—recognition as the most influential person in the academy to assist the cadets in graduating. They said I assisted in every way: sharing notes, leading teams, training groups after hours, and volunteering.

I worked for the city as a volunteer for four years, winning the Reserve Officer of the Year Award two of those four years, and donating more than two thousand hours of service, which was more hours—almost double—than any other reserve in that period.

I trained with the detectives' SWAT team and other specialties. I was given several honorable mentions and commendations from sergeants, lieutenants, and commanders for things like working extra hours, going above and beyond for the department, and for receiving compliments from citizens. It was very important that while working for the department you maintained an elevated level of professionalism. The public did not know the difference between a volunteer and a full-time officer. Reserves at my high level carried weapons, drove our own vehicles, and basically executed most daily duties as regular full-time officers. I assisted regularly in training with full-time and reserve officers and volunteered for years at the reserve academy when the new recruits arrived. I also had a chance to work with kids while on patrol—sometimes ones who shared similar circumstances to mine growing up. I felt a connection with them and enjoyed making a difference in their lives, even if only for a few moments. I particularly cherished the Shop with a Cop community program where we took underprivileged children shopping for Christmas and enjoyed playing in the charity basketball games. We had lots of positive and fulfilling interaction with the community.

FINDING MENTORS AND STAYING ON TRACK

There are mentors all around us and most of them are dying to teach, share, and help others grow. I was taught by some of the mentors in my life because of opening myself up to that engagement. In other words, I was very talkative and asked lots of questions to people I met. I always show a real and honest interest in what people have to say and as a result they keep talking and advising and teaching me, maybe without even knowing it. To this day I ask people I encounter what they do for a living and I strike up business conversations whenever possible. But I learn from nonbusiness encounters as well. Whatever you do, keep asking and talking, listening and learning.

Now I have assisted in mentoring a few people through the Tacoma Rescue Mission—a faith-based nonprofit that houses both recovering addicts and the homeless, plus feeds more than one thousand people in need per day. Some of these people have had very difficult challenges in their lives, but after they achieve recovery, the one thing usually missing is structure or support after the fact. Myself and others spend time with a handful of these individuals, mentoring them on how to be productive employees or even possibly becoming business owners themselves. We take the time to answer their phone calls and take questions, listen to their struggles, and most of all give honest business advice. I've been told by one of these individuals that this has been life-changing for him. After his graduation he climbed Mount Rainier at 14,411 feet. He's written and performed Christian rap songs. He's lost seventy-five pounds and is raising his daughters while he sets a good example for them as a solid, reliable employee. He's done all this and is firmly on his way to realizing his dreams. He is truly an inspiration and an example of how mentors can make a difference in someone's life who otherwise may have no one.

Mentors are great because they are usually someone you hold in high regard—someone you look up to, aspire to be, or at least learn from. They force you to elevate your way of thinking and put you in the best position to succeed. We all fall offtrack and lose our way from time to time. And anything worth having will generally require lots of work and accountability. If you are pretty good at measuring yourself and tracking progress, great. But if not, ask someone you look up to what they do to achieve their goals, and I'm sure they will be willing to share. They may even work with you to achieve your goals or at least help keep you inspired and on track.

OVERCOMING FEAR

When I partnered up with Nick as a marketing specialist team and moved in with him, we naturally began to hang out more. Nick was a bit of an adrenaline junkie, to say the least, who enjoyed rock and mountain climbing, sky diving, scuba diving, skiing, etc.—all things that terrified me. Nick is the main reason I began to challenge and overcome some of the fear I had developed at an early age. He had a fantastic way of teaching and showing me how to shift my paradigm, which means changing the way

I saw something from fear's warped perception to what it actually was.

Let me give you a few examples.

I had a terrible experience when I tried skiing for the first time and was injured on a black-diamond-level ski run. For ten years I never tried it again. Nick, an avid skier, was very patient and took me through the small runs and explained the progression of learning how to ski. After one year and twelve ski days, I was skiing the black-diamond runs, and eventually double-black-diamonds runs.

My trust in Nick helped me to overcome the fear of skiing. Nick then encouraged me to overcome my lifelong fear of heights. At first I told him he was crazy and there was no way I was climbing rocks with ropes. Eventually he talked me into hiking in an area of Washington called Index, where there is a twenty-foot rock climbers can rappel off. He brought the gear in his backpack and said, "Here is where I teach you to rappel."

Glancing all the way up the rock, I said, "No way." But after about thirty minutes and a lot of friendly harassment/encouragement, I was standing on the edge of that rock with twenty feet of air and Nick holding the rope line below.

I can only describe the physical fear I felt as: "I'm about to lose my life and it's *on purpose*." I was sweating, shaking, and so nervous. It took me at least thirty more minutes to step to the edge and go over with my back facing the ground. But as I worked my way down the rock face, I will never forget the feeling of exhilaration. I was finally free of what was a crippling fear of heights, and my confidence was through the roof.

Nick taught me that it's okay to be fearful, but you must control it and understand that the fear is all about the unknown and not reality. He taught me how to trust my training, abilities, and the gear I was using.

After learning how to rappel, Nick and I went on to climb lots of rocks and mountains. We crossed glaciers and crevasses, including climbing most of the volcanos in the Northwest. These mountains included the tallest in Washington State, Mount Rainier, at 14,411 feet. I really felt like I could do anything in the world once I hit that peak. It's so challenging, beautiful, peaceful, and humbling when you're at the top.

BONUS POINT: Don't let fear, naysayers, bullies, or anyone hold you back. Surround yourself with people who push you and drive you to improve. Do this and you will achieve truly amazing things.

RELATIONSHIPS—FINDING THE RIGHT PERSON

It takes a very special person willing to sacrifice time and energy to be in a relationship with an entrepreneur. If you're like me, you will need to find a partner that is patient and understands what drives you. I dedicate a lot of time to my craft and if I did not have the right partner in my life my marriage would be on a path to failure.

So how and when did I find the right one?

I met Christina, who would eventually become my wife, when I first lived in Washington State. I was new to the state, lonely, and wanted to start dating. I did not have any issues talking to people, but I had time constraints based on my work schedule. And where do you meet people when you're twenty-five anyway? A friend of mine in the same business told me about Match.com and that he was meeting all kinds of girls on the site. He too kept a crazy schedule, so I thought I would give it a try. Admittedly, I was very skeptical at first because then it was a relatively new way of meeting people—so much so that others I mentioned it to made fun of it and discouraged me from meeting people there. At the time I only knew one person who had ever used the site, so I was on the fence. But I took a leap of faith and gave it a go.

Within one week of joining, I was getting dozens of "winks" and e-mails from several women and began to quickly understand the site's value. What would have taken hours and at least $50 to $100 at a club per night could be accomplished in ten minutes, basically for free. Plus, you could partake from the comfort of your own home whenever you wanted. It seemed too good to be true. This was exactly what I needed, because it kept me out of clubs and allowed me to focus on work yet still socialize. I had some great conversations and met some really nice women. It's funny—people are so afraid of the unknown and that keeps them from realizing the wonderful things that await them on the other side.

One night I messaged this person and after some terribly misspelled correspondence on my part and a lot of schmoozing and courting, I finally landed a date with this beautiful girl. The date would prove to be very important to my future. She became a tremendous support and source of love and connection. Later, she stood by me, traveling back and forth to Oregon every weekend during the challenging time I ran the store.

Christina and I were together for seven years and engaged for two before we got married in October of 2010, so we really understood each other. Christina is a good person and a hard worker with deep family values. She developed her skills through working up to three jobs at a time at an early age and by getting a master's degree. These skills and degree would eventually help her build a lengthy career and earn a management position in human resources. Our values and work ethics are aligned—a great recipe for success. Getting married was wonderful and fulfilling in many ways, but something I had not realized until I was in a stable relationship was that it allowed me to focus on my career, personal growth, and development more than ever before. Christina was also a considerable influence on me working to build up the relationships with my family members, as I was then distant from most of them. I did not have my personal priorities straight.

Don't get me wrong, we've had our ups and downs while dating and through marriage, but with effective communication and an understanding of the other person's perspective, you can solve a lot of problems and move forward. I recommend the book *Men Are from Mars, Women Are from Venus* by John Gray. It's an informative read for couples and will certainly give you a better understanding of each other.

BONUS POINT: Taking a significant amount of time to select the right someone to share your life with is very important because it will likely shape the future successes in your personal and professional lives. If you have someone who understands you and supports your choices, but is also objective and pushes back when needed, it can be of great value to keep you on track.

One of the relationships I worked on after meeting Christina is the one with my maternal grandpa, Harley. My grandpa worked hard as an RV and mobile home builder for more than forty years, and then worked part-time well into his seventies. At least once a year I make sure to spend time with him and I'm glad I do. I love hearing his stories. He has always saved his money and lived below his means. This foresight has served him well and allows him to live a happy, independent, single life. Had I spent more time with him at a younger age, he would have been an inspiration, but we lived eight hundred miles apart. Now he always talks about saving and it's funny because he's 100 percent right. If only I had caught on earlier.

BONUS POINT: I recommend spending as much time with your family as you can, especially with those who are much older and have paved the way for all of us today. They are a wealth of knowledge and love to share it. If you do not have family around, find the seniors in your community and spark up a conversation. Most of them would love it and you will be amazed at what you will learn while likely enriching their lives.

PERSONAL RELATIONSHIPS

Building relationships with my clients and business associates has made a significant difference in my sales career. Taking the time to understand where people are coming from and what motivates or discourages them is very important if you want to help, sell to, or just be an influencer. I've also taken many of the tools I learned in business and applied them to my personal relationships with my wife, friends, and family. It takes time to earn trust, and if you work on yourself first, then you will be better equipped to deal with issues with others that arise.

Let's say you're in a relationship and constantly fighting about something. You must learn to take the emotion out of it and just work on the facts, character, and values of the person on the other side. This will give you both clarity as to what the deeper issue is and usually get you to a resolution. Really work to understand that person's perspective and then be very clear on explaining yours, based on facts and truth rather than emotion. It may be hard to find but somewhere in the middle there is compromise.

NEGOTIATING AND BUILDING WEALTH

When I was thirty-seven years old, I resigned from the police reserves to focus on some new opportunities. After four years' growth, my company had double-digit increases—and that was all while also working for the police department. I would work my day job and then work a swing or graveyard shift only to do it again later in the week. Instead of feeling overwhelmed, this crazy schedule improved my output. I became very efficient, reading books on how to improve and cut waste out of my life.

People always ask me, "How do you do all the stuff you do?" And I reply, "I don't know; I just do what I do." Most of what I've accomplished is from sheer determination and grit, not mind tricks. I believe most people know what they *need* to do, but lack the support or structure to stay on track to keep doing it.

Let's talk for a minute about negotiating and how important it is to building wealth. I have negotiated the following and it has paid off big:

- Bought several homes in distress or in foreclosure, savings tens of thousands.
- Negotiated and shopped my dental work once, saving thousands.
- Bought many cars for others with cash and shipped them from all over the county, saving thousands.
- I once drove cars all over town—from car dealership to car dealership—using the vehicle from the previous lot as a negotiation tool for a family member's purchase, saving thousands.
- I negotiated a friend's vehicle from impound from $500 down to $50. (Actually, it was negotiated down to nothing, but I made my friend pony up the $50 for the small locally owned impound lot as a courtesy.)

- I collected thousands of dollars from a large corporation that was brushing off my small business owner friend after a year with no payments for his services, all through negotiations.
- I was paid $23,000 for making a five-minute phone call. Unbelievable.

These are just some of the negotiations that saved me or my friends and family countless thousands throughout the years. All this was done through conversation, research, and sheer determination. You must be willing to outwork the person on the other side and if you do, you will most likely win, or at least eventually find someone you will beat on the product you are negotiating.

I read a book called *Secrets of the Millionaire Mind* by T. Harv Eker and one valuable insight that stood out to me was when he talked about wealth. He said rich people focus on net worth and poor people focus on their working income. I had been working for years on cutting expenses and saving, but this book really laid out the mindset you must adopt to create wealth.

HOW SAVING ON VEHICLES PROPELLED MY REAL-ESTATE INVESTING PORTFOLIO

In a moment of weakness, I bought a truck as a second vehicle. I purchased it because I found that many of the projects I worked on needed a truck, but I may have gone a little overboard. You see I had it shipped from across the country because cars on the West Coast were running a lot higher for some reason. I bought it under value but after a few years found that I was not using it as much as I thought I would. It was a nice truck that I had added several upgrades to, so the value was high. I think when all was said and done I still owed about $22,000 on it and it was worth about $40,000. I was trying to figure out if I should keep it or sell it, but then had to go on a business trip for two weeks and decided to deal with it when I got back.

One of my favorite things to do while traveling is to network and discuss all aspects of business with colleagues and anyone willing to share thoughts and ideas. While at dinner one night with my good friend Pat, we ended up discussing the difference between investing in the stock market and real estate. I'd known Pat for more than ten years, but the conversation only came up because I was asking Pat lots of questions about his personal life and he shared. We went back and forth giving examples of how one investment strategy might be better than the other. Pat invested in real estate but was new at it. On the other hand, his father was a stocks guy. I only knew about stock investing and was depositing a fixed amount into a T. Rowe Price mutual funds or index funds account. But to be honest, I only knew that I deposited every month and not much more beyond that.

We did a deep dive into the ROI (return on investment) for each investment, using napkins to scribble equation numbers. Afterward, I could not ignore the returns on buying real estate and the flexibility it would give, but I needed to learn more.

BONUS POINT: It's all right to chat about the daily gossip, what the neighbor is doing, or workplace drama if that's what you're into. But if you can spark conversations about things in life that you can *learn from*, or with people that are successful at something, then maybe you, too, can learn and excel from the other person's experience. It's my opinion most people spend way too much time with gossip, watching TV, or playing video games to ever see what opportunities are out there in front of them.

So I'm on my business trip and all I could think about was the real-estate conversation I had with Pat. I owned my own home but never really understood the power of investment it offered. As soon as I got back I bought the five most popular real-estate investing books at the time and read them all in four months. I began calculating the numbers, mapping the state and areas of opportunity to buy, building spreadsheets to show how I could make a profit in the worst-case scenario, and started building my plan to get into real estate.

Pat and I discussed the idea of each buying a house, fixing it up, and renting it. We also proposed buying, fixing, and then selling them.

At the time of this venture, about 2014, I had a modest net worth and really no direction for my investments other than to keep making my monthly stocks deposit and adding to savings. One of the series of books I read, The Millionaire Real Estate Investor series by Gary Keller, Dave Jenks, and Jay Papasan, really laid out a blueprint to search and eventually buy a good rental property, so I started there. I was well aware that even though I read expert books and had been given all this advice from others, there was no guarantee that this would work. I still had to build out my own personal strategy that I was comfortable with.

It seems like there are a lot of seminars and presenters selling concepts that worked for them, but many that I've read about or attended do not include much content about the individuals who they are trying to teach. No matter what you are told, remember it's critical that you, as an individual, be highly motivated and inspired, but that you also need to find a way to be successful in your own space and circumstances, not necessarily how someone else did it. There are a ton of good self-help seminars and books out there, but you must put a lot of time into formulating your own plan of attack. If you don't get caught up in one strategy or go down a rabbit hole you cannot get out of, you will mitigate your risk of failure significantly.

BONUS POINT: I find that when I drive or the time I spend at the gym gives me the opportunity to listen to audio books and podcasts. This is a fantastic way to use otherwise wasted time to educate yourself. Most gyms offer free Wi-Fi, so you have no excuse start learning.

MY FIRST INVESTMENT PROPERTY

I saved approximately $55,000 from driving the Lexus the next five years after it was paid off. I realized because of the lifestyle I was living, and with little to no debt, it made no sense to let my money sit in savings, making me less than .5 percent. I really wanted my money working for me, not the other way around.

My goal was to find a property that I could buy with 20 percent down (to avoid the extra cost of mortgage insurance) and finance the rest. I figured a $100,000 house with 20 percent down would leave me with a mortgage payment—including taxes and insurance—of about $600. This would leave me a budget to renovate if needed of

$20,000 to $25,000. I'd then rent the house out. At these numbers, I knew I could make a profit. Next, I analyzed the market in several areas around me and found that there were only a few offering homes in my desired price range. This is where I think some people make a mistake when trying to invest in rentals—either they rent their own home because they want to move and think they can make money as a result (breaking even if they are lucky), or they buy a property to rent where they want to live instead of where the market or their circumstances tell them to buy.

I verified both the average price of rental units in the area and the vacancy rates and they were favorable. The home would need to rent for at least $995 per month. Several of my friends questioned the market I selected, but the data I gathered—and my own personal comfort level—informed me this was the right place for me to start. The chosen area was a one-hour drive from my house, and I knew I would have to drive back and forth a lot, but I was determined to make it work. After checking out ten properties, I found the perfect property—an REO property (real estate owned, aka bank-owned foreclosure) with minimal renovations needed for $100,000—and bought it. This is not a real-estate book, so I will fast forward though most of the details, but I want to highlight a few things:

- I spent six weeks working on this property with a few temp helpers. I drove my small trailer full of tools that I bought for this project back and forth at night and on weekends until the project was finished—sometimes working sixteen-hour days, including my regular job.

- I invested about $20,000 in updates. Most were not necessary, but I wanted the house to be in selling condition, not just rental condition.

- I learned most of the updating skills on YouTube and estimate that I saved about $30,000 by doing a lot of it myself.

- My all-in investment was about $45,000, which included closing costs, down payment, and renovations.

- I rented the home in less than a week for $1,100 on a three-year lease.

- Taxes, mortgage, plus insurance came to about $620 a month.

- My monthly cash flow after accounting for vacancy and maintenance was about $350.

- I sold the house three years later for $165,000 and had a balance due of about $74,000 on the mortgage.

After three years, I had a total investment of $45,000 in the home. My final gross profit was $12,000 on the rental income and $81,000 on the sale of the house after the real-estate fees. If you take the $12,000 plus $81,000 and deduct my original $45,000, I had a profit of $48,000 when all was said and done. Now that may not sound like a lot but look at it this way.

For a little sacrifice of my time renovating for six weeks and driving the same car for five extra years, I had a return on my investment of roughly 30 percent per year using the money I saved on the Lexus payment. Historically, the average stocks in the market or real estate show you a return of 5 to 8 percent, so not bad for my first house. I also had the freedom of using the monthly cash flow if I needed it and a few tax write-offs. Keep in mind these are rough numbers but they're close. There's a little interest to account for, as well as market trends, but it's still a really good return.

Throughout the process, I stayed true to my original plan. Many people I worked around asked why was I buying there or bothering to fix things because it was just a rental. But by sticking to my plan and putting the work in upfront, I saved lots of time, money, and headache later.

Per my research, I wisely bought in one of the better areas, not only netting me a higher rental rate, but also a higher and quicker selling price. And by repairing and updating things along the way, I *added* value.

This was my first investment property, so I'm sure it was not executed perfectly. I may have made even more money had I done it differently. But I learned a lot and made money on the deal. I took action when I was given the information. You can't overcome fear and eventually win if you don't get out and try. I'm not going to sugarcoat this. There *are* many risks and it's really hard work, but five months prior I had no idea this was even possible. I did it, so there is no reason you can't do it too. Just remember, it starts with a few key principles:

- Passion, enthusiasm, and determination.
- Hard work and then *more* hard work.
- Educate yourself with mentors and books.
- Absolutely eliminate the words "I can't" and "fear" out of your thought process.
- Sacrifice—you must give up some of your free time and maybe some of the finer things in life, but just for a while.

BONUS POINT: When I apply for a loan, I have all my documentation ready—sometimes up to fifty documents. When I first started I would use spreadsheets to illustrate my plans. I always draw up examples or define my future goals. All this sets you apart from most people. This puts you in a good light and more people will want to do business with you or work with you. Always overprepare and outwork those you're competing with. It's so important to be ready in life. Whether you are interviewing for a job, buying a piece of property, or presenting a business plan, do your research and overprepare. If you make it easy for the people you are trying to do business with, they may give you a chance. Sometimes they will even overlook other shortcomings. In my case, I never had any formal education, but I super prepared for interviews, building myself up bigger than I was on paper using preparation, attitude, and carefully placed confidence. I knew so much about the people and/or companies I was interviewing with, I could tell they knew I valued the opportunity. Be personable and genuine. Have some positive energy about you. That behind-the-scenes work and hustle really made a difference as I stumbled through life.

Another great resource I found after buying my first few properties is BiggerPockets.com. On this site, there are many terrific books available, plus forums to share thoughts and ideas. There are even some nice tools to calculate the value of a real-estate purchase. I highly recommend joining its free basic membership. If I had only found them earlier, it could have saved me *lots of time* building spreadsheets. BiggerPockets also hosts regular podcast and webinar interviews with fascinating entrepreneurs. I now follow several and continue to learn from them all. Two of my favorites are *The Tim Ferriss Show* and *How I Built This with Guy Raz*. Check them out.

Regarding sacrifice, a new neighbor once asked me what I did for a living. "All I see of you is work, work, work," he said, referring to my nonstop hustling.

"I take considerable pride in my property and want to maintain it at a high level of quality," I said to him. "I also run several businesses and to keep them profitable I must keep moving, outpacing the competition, and always improving. I work as though someone is coming up from behind to take what I've earned, and I will never let that happen."

He and I had a good discussion about retirement, as he was close to it. I told him that retiring on my terms was a priority to me and to achieve the financial freedom to do that meant I had to sacrifice time now. (That is *if* I ever fully retire.) He understood and said that he wished he would have thought of that himself at a younger age. He then asked if I would be interested in doing some business in the future with him. See—another possible opportunity right in front of me by being personable and hustling.

The truth is I'm the kind of person who enjoys helping people with their challenges and problem-solving. Business associates and friends often ask me for advice on a wide range of topics. After solving a particularly challenging issue for one of my clients, he said, "If I was stranded on an island and there was only one other person that I could have with me to get us off that island, it would be *you*."

"Why me?" I asked.

He told me it was because he knew I would do whatever it would take to get us off the island. And without a doubt, I *would* eventually succeed.

I wear that compliment like a badge of honor. I work hard for my business, my team, and my clients for a reason, and I really appreciate the recognition. These comments mean I'm doing something right. When people stop talking about you, start worrying.

CITY OF HOPE AND AN UNBELIEVABLE GIFT

I've learned a lot about business while working as an independent contractor for Ashley Furniture Industries. They are very passionate about continuous improvement, producing a quality product, cutting costs, and making a profit. I'm amazed at how dedicated they are to these values and mission. The work ethic the owners display is inspiring and definitely has had a profound impact on the strategies I've used while building my own business. Since working as an independent contractor, the company has grown from $900 million to more than $6 billion, and become the number one furniture company in the U.S., so you can imagine how hard they and everyone around them, including all the independent contractors and factory employees, work every day. They have also had an influence on me with the charitable contributions they make—inspiring me to give back too.

I had the honor of flying with executives from Ashley Furniture Industries on one of the company's planes to major research institution City of Hope's home base in Southern California. There they donated $50 million to help cure type 1 diabetes and were honored with their name being placed on a building. I was brought along because I had worked with City of Hope on some of my own charity fund-raising events and the company I represented appreciated that work. It was truly one of the most amazing experiences of my life. We toured the facility and spent the day talking with the actual doctors and researchers working on not just the cure for diabetes, but cancer and other terrible ailments. It was a once-in-a-lifetime event that I will never forget it.

I know I've said this before, but anything is possible. I was living on my own at the age of fifteen. I have no formal education. I built my career by talking, and now I'm flying on a private jet with the owners of a multibillion-dollar company who are donating so much money to a cause that it's sure to make a difference. This family business is an inspiration and I'm so thankful to have spent time with them. I can't even begin to imagine the positive impact they've had on the tens of thousands of lives and organizations they've touched.

MY SECOND INVESTMENT PROPERTY

Six months later, I bought another rental property five blocks from the first.

Remember that truck I bought to help renovate my first investment property? I listed the truck and estimated that if I could net $15,000 to invest, plus use some additional money from the savings generated by driving my old Lexus, I might have enough to buy another rental property.

I sold it within a week and was ready to start investing.

I bought this second rental house property for $99,000 and added $10,000 in upgrades. With my down payment, I had invested $34,000 total. I rented this one for $995 a month on a two-year lease and its cash flow was about $250 per month. I basically took a vehicle that was costing me about $500 per month in payments and insurance and turned it into a rental property that was making me $250 per month while someone else paid down my mortgage.

Later, one of the best real-estate deals I bought was where I paid only the $50,000 back taxes owed on it. Three years later that house was worth $240,000. This crazy opportunity was referred to me by a family member who knew I bought real estate.

Within four years, I had quadrupled my net worth to more than seven figures, using real estate and a little support from the stock market. Reaching this was the goal I had set six years earlier. I knew if I could reach this goal before the age of forty-five—giving me several years before my target retirement age—it would put me in a position of financial freedom at a young enough age to decide how I want to retire versus circumstances dictating it.

I reached it by age forty.

THE TONY ROBBINS EFFECT

I've attended several of Tony Robbins's seminars and think he is simply amazing. I can't begin to tell you how influential he is to so many people. There's a misconception that he's simply a motivator, pitching smoke and mirrors—a guru of sorts. Maybe to some, but he is much more than that; he is an inspiration, a healer, a survivor, a mentor, a teacher, a business developer, an investor, and father to name a few. I have not met Tony Robbins, but did high-five him once and have learned a lot from him through the years. At a recent seminar for business management and development, he talked about the importance of hiring a financial advisor. I did that the minute I got home, and his advice and what I learned from that advisor saved me about $4,000 per year at a minimum.

NO GUARANTEES

I can't tell you exactly how I've achieved my position in life. And if I knew, I don't know if telling you would make a difference in yours. I say this because one thing I've learned about people through my journey is that we all require different motivations, incentives, support systems, and circumstances to help us get to our individual definition of success. I do believe that everyone has it in them to get what they want out of life if they work at it. Find what inspires you to be great and surround yourself with what that looks like. Think about a time in your life that you had any kind of success and use that energy to drive you to reach this new goal.

Today I'm a partner or investor in several businesses, I have a healthy but modest real-estate portfolio that will continue to thrive. I save approximately 35 to 40 percent of my income every month and am happily married. I'm a mountain climber and an Advanced Rescue Scuba Diver. I have big goals and am always driving forward and measuring to stay on track. I hold myself accountable so no one else has to. I donate my time and money every year to support causes I believe in and that's very rewarding.

I'm a firm believer that when you teach you learn. I have held hundreds and hundreds of sales training courses for tens of thousands of sales associates, and sold several hundred million dollars' worth of products and services. I have mentored people through their financial challenges and helped people build up or even start their businesses. There has been nothing more rewarding in my life than the day I got married and the time spent when I'm giving back to others or my community. I can't wait to see what the future holds!

It would be an understatement to say that my sales career, investing in myself, and an unrelenting belief that I can do anything I set my mind to, has afforded me an incredible life far better than I could have ever imagined.

FINAL THOUGHTS

W E ARE ALL the same when we start, but if we are not careful our environment and circumstances can alter who we become. You must make a choice early in life on who you want to be and make the commitment to be that person, because it's likely no one will just give it to you. This will take more work than you can see at the time, but I promise that you will do things you never thought possible and develop into your best self if you commit. Trust in the process.

Look at me:

- I could not piece enough cash together with several unreliable part-time jobs, so I used what I was good at and threw some parties that made me two weeks' wages in four days. I had no goal of being the best party thrower of all time.

- I earned my way into a sales position by working *for free* on a sales floor—not even the store I originally worked at for free, but for the same manager who saw my willingness to do whatever it took. He hired me at a different store years later. I had no intention of working for free indefinitely or being the greatest salesman on earth.

- I was the most effective hotdog cart server without even knowing it because I was an effective people person. The attitude and enthusiasm I used there landed me a job with the number one influencer and mentor of my life. I never aspired to own my own hotdog cart or be the best hotdog cart operator.

- I started investing in real estate, growing my net worth by four times, by being curious, asking lots of questions, and investing in myself. I surrounded myself with the kind of people I aspired to be like. I had no vision of being the number one real-estate investor in the country.

The secret to my success is no secret. It can be adopted by anyone who's willing to work hard and set reasonable, achievable goals. I strive to improve and expand my knowledge in everything I do. Much of the time I find some form of success when setting a goal, but it's *my* success, not someone else's. Never feel like you are failing because you measure yourself against someone else or because you don't reach that goal by 100 percent. You get up and you continue.

I leave you with these proven keys to success:

- Set goals and check them early and often, refining your process as you work toward the result.
- Work harder than anyone around you. It will pay off.
- Be personable and ask lots of questions of those you respect.
- Take criticism and failure to heart and improve from them. Don't take it personally or get down on yourself.
- Don't listen to naysayers and negative people, as there is only so much time to build your ideal life and they will get in your way.
- Surround yourself with people who will challenge you—forcing you to rise to their level and telling you what you may not want to hear.
- Live below your means and create multiple streams of income. When your income goes up, save it. Don't spend it unless you're investing.

Looking back, what I didn't have growing up, didn't matter. It's what I did with what I had that made all the difference.

CHRIS ROBERTS

ACKNOWLEDGMENTS

I want to thank my wife, Christina, for having the patience to put up with my crazy ways, countless long hours, and constant business talk for the last eight years of marriage. If not for her dedication to our relationship, and constantly proofing my work, this book would not be possible. I love you and appreciate your support.

Thank you to my mother, Donna Arnold, for keeping me on the right path the first fourteen years of my life. And thanks to my dad, Tom Roberts, for at least trying for a while. I love you both.

Thanks to the rest of the family—Aunt Cindy, Aunt Vicki, Grandpa Harley, Grandma Cleone, and Uncle Rick—who at times pulled together as needed to make it work.

A shout-out to all the good friends, like Travis Gilinsky, Tyler Hebert, Pat Roos, and many others, who I spent years with, plotting and planning a better life and a higher purpose. From my early years, I want to give a special shout-out to Roy Rush, Matt Hurtado, Marshall

Bauerfeind. and the bike-riding crew (Mike, Tim, Chris, and Ryan). If not for each of your friendships, I don't know how I would have made it through at such a young age.

In the humblest way, I can't thank enough the mentors in my life, like Ron and Margie Norgan, Steve Wilcox, and Miguel Stansberry among others, for changing the way I see the world and business. You are making a difference.

Thanks to Ashley Furniture Industries for indirectly carving me into a business professional and inspiring me to be more charitable, because giving back is one of the greatest rewards in life.

To Patrick Price, thank you for developing my personal story into an enjoyable book. You're a gifted editor.

To Lauren Forte, thank you for the expert copyediting.

To my cover designer, Krista Vossen, thank you for giving my book its memorable face.

And lastly, I want to thank all the people who challenged me or did not believe achieving dreams was possible—those who put me down or set up roadblocks for me to break through and people who judged without getting to know me—if not for you, my true potential would not have been realized.

ABOUT THE AUTHOR

Born in Orange, California and raised by a single mother, Chris Roberts moved to southern Oregon at the age of fourteen. On his own at a very young age, where opportunities were limited, Chris developed a strong drive that came from the daily challenges of growing up with little to nothing. He found himself jumping into things that seemed impossible, and made them possible.

Throughout Chris's life, he worked up to three jobs at a time to survive, inspired and determined to work hard for a better life. He realized at an early age that he had a passion for working with people and found his calling in sales and marketing. Through hard work and perseverance, Chris became a young business owner and entrepreneur. He is currently the president of Fusion Sales and Marketing, Inc., owner of Fusion Properties, and co-owner of High Trek POS. Chris also had the honor of serving as a reserve police officer in Lacey, Washington for four years and received multiple service awards for his dedication and time. He is an avid reader, a mentor, a mountain climber, and a scuba diver.

Chris and his wife, Christina, are equally passionate about working, volunteering, and giving back—most recently working with the Tacoma Rescue Mission. Both devoted animal lovers, their family includes three dogs: Oliver, Bentley, and recently adopted Devo.

Chris has been through many challenges and struggles growing up and understands the difficulties that people face. He is thankful for the opportunity to give back and is dedicated to changing lives.

60138782R00107

Made in the USA
Columbia, SC
15 June 2019